ELIZA ORME'S AMBITIONS

Eliza Orme's Ambitions

Politics and the Law in Victorian London

Leslie Howsam

OpenBook
Publishers

https://www.openbookpublishers.com
©2024 Leslie Howsam

Any digital material and resources associated with this volume will be available at https://doi.org/10.11647/OBP.0392#resources

ISBN Paperback: 978-1-80511-233-4
ISBN Hardback: 978-1-80511-234-1
ISBN Digital (PDF): 978-1-80511-235-8
ISBN Digital eBook (EPUB): 978-1-80511-236-5
ISBN XML: 978-1-80511-237-2
ISBN HTML: 978-1-80511-238-9

DOI: 10.11647/OBP.0392

Cover illustration: Eliza Orme (1889, The Cameron Studio), ©The estate of Jenny Loxton Young. Background: Sketchepedia / Freepik
Cover design by Jeevanjot Kaur Nagpal

Contents

About the Author

Leslie Howsam is a Fellow of the Royal Society of Canada (FRSC) and Emerita Distinguished University Professor at the University of Windsor in Canada; she is Senior Research Fellow in the Centre for Digital Humanities at Toronto Metropolitan University. Leslie was a founding member of the Society for the History of Authorship, Reading, and Publishing (SHARP) and served as its president 2009 to 2013. Her most recent book is the *Cambridge Companion to the History of the Book* (2015), while her best-known book is *Old Books & New Histories: An Orientation to Studies in Book and Print Culture* (2006). For further information please see https://lesliehowsam.ca

List of Illustrations

Prologue

Eliza Orme was a rarity in Victorian Britain, an independent single woman in public life. Academically trained in law but excluded from formal practice, she forged a precarious career on the fringes of the patriarchal legal community and used that as a springboard for energetic involvement in party politics. She lived, and worked, and made her mark in the last quarter of the nineteenth century in Britain. After that, she was more or less forgotten, until I got curious, remained interested, eventually came to understand why and how her story had disappeared from history, and finally wrote this book. It is my story almost as much as hers, and it is not a biography, because even after half a lifetime the author still does not know enough about the subject to write what is known as 'the definitive work'. (Perhaps no one will ever know enough about this elusive figure.) Instead, this is a research memoir, which allows me to integrate my own research adventure with an account of Eliza Orme's private life and public career, and to ask what it is about her that has intrigued me for some forty years. As for what it is about me that lets me speak for her—I am a historian, and one who takes joy in using the documents to be found in archives and libraries. But I also know that much of what happened in the past—especially to women—was never documented, or the documents were lost, or got buried among someone else's papers. I have discovered a lot, and recognized some connections, and finally allowed myself to speculate about her motives and her ambitions.

When Eliza Orme set about challenging the deeply patriarchal profession of law as practiced in Britain—at the remarkably early date of 1872—one of the reasons was that she believed nothing would assist the cause of women's suffrage so much as practical work done by women. This was typical, She once told an audience, 'I am hopelessly practical'. Her approach to being an agent of change meant getting things done,

     https://doi.org/10.11647/OBP.0392.00

rather than rising into clouds of rhetoric about the causes she supported. Still less did she talk to people about her private hopes and dreams, perhaps for a brilliant career in public life. Instead she set about testing the limits of what could be done. Other women who espoused the same causes as she did were not noticeably practical; they were visionaries, and now they're celebrated as the leaders of Britain's contemporary campaigns for women's suffrage, for career opportunities, for all those crucial reforms. Perhaps that's why they are remembered, while Orme was all but forgotten until—as this book recounts—a chance encounter in a Canadian university seminar room somehow ignited decades of research. Orme was, it turns out, a remarkable woman: not only practical, but ambitious, competent, well-connected, witty, generous, and a strategist. What she wasn't, however, was England's first woman barrister or solicitor; those achievements happened almost half a century later, to other people. She wasn't the iniquitous anti-women's-suffrage schemer of some of her contemporaries' jealous imaginations, either. Formidable competence and relentless practicality, it turns out, are not always appreciated by the visionaries.

So, who was Eliza Orme? I have spent almost forty years following her traces through books, magazines, and newspapers preserved in libraries, and through handwritten records in archives. For most of that time, there was almost no information, not even a photograph, and I was too busy with other things to do much with what I did know. Now, with both retirement leisure and digital search engines at my disposal, I have learned enough to change the question. I know who she was, especially her public persona—first woman in England to earn a law degree (in 1888 at the age of thirty-nine); powerful behind-the-scenes strategist for the women's branch of the Liberal Party; a key figure in factory inspection and prison reform; active in Anglo-Irish politics; part of the first wave of the feminist movement; a journalist and public speaker who addressed women's work, their financial independence and their right to vote. I know what she did for a living, too, though that's hard to describe because it's complicated, implausible, and somewhat disheartening. Totally and irrevocably excluded from the practice of law either as a barrister or a solicitor, she set up a business at the fringes of those professions, discreetly preparing legal paperwork and charging a hefty fee for the service. (Her clients were credentialed men who commissioned her services privately in order to publicly claim her labours as their own.) And she had other side hustles and gig jobs, albeit presenting herself in a much more dignified way than those words suggest, but I use them to stress that she was a precursor of today's precarious labour economy. More on that later, but for now the question has to change, to ask whose she is, beginning with whose she was—how her colleagues, friends, family, admirers, detractors, clients, competitors and protégées all measured an outsized personality against their own needs and ambitions. Further, whose academic or cultural research quarry is she now? What do twenty-first century lawyers and legal-history scholars make of her anomalous position with respect to a stringently regulated professional status? Are historians of the first wave of feminism ready to accept her as one of that number, despite a strategic position on the suffrage question that set her apart from her peers? Is her adventurous personal life of interest to readers more attracted to the woman than the legal pioneer?

Most of all, she was her own woman. Eliza Orme was independently single and financially secure, at a time when marital status pretty much defined identity for women and earning a comfortable self-sufficient living was very rare. She came from a large, loving, prosperous and supportive family from whom she inherited a talent for friendship and a sense of security that let her be combative in encounters with people she disagreed with. She was often funny, and I think she was probably a lot of fun to spend time with. She had one very close lifelong companion who was both a fellow-student and a family friend, later a business partner, and eventually the executor of her estate. That was Reina Emily Lawrence. It is reasonable to speculate that theirs was an intimate relationship, the kind that was acceptable in advanced social circles at the time as long as it was not made explicit. There is no hard evidence for this idea, but neither have I found a scrap of evidence that she had any love affairs with men.

This book is about Eliza Orme, but it is also about me. I have written it partly to figure out why I remain intrigued with her story, even after spending decades researching and teaching a different branch of British history. Like me, like most people with a reputation, she was a public figure whose private side was accessible only to those she trusted. And like almost everyone, neither Orme nor the people close to her obliged posterity by leaving very many records of that private side behind. Having said that, though, I am going to start with two remarkable bits of historical evidence—both of them I discovered quite recently—one that shows the public Miss Orme, LL.B. another offering a glimpse of the private Eliza.

The public person was well known for being a divisive figure in the Women's Liberal Federation—or as an anonymous newspaper article called them, 'a group of Liberal dames'. On 3 March 1892, an article in The *British Weekly* suggested, rather snidely, that a book might someday be written about such anomalous political figures. The imagined book, an epic poem, would solve a contemporary conundrum about Eliza Orme: 'In that serio-comic epic which must surely one day depict to the world the story of the early days of the women's Liberal movement, it is an entertaining matter for conjecture which of Miss Orme's two reputations the poet will find most convenient for his artistic purposes'. She had adversaries within the Federation, so-called 'progressives', who aspired to force their party to start accepting women's suffrage as a matter of policy and felt thwarted by her insistence on more circumspect tactics. To those people, Miss Orme was 'the arch-villain, the malignant schemer, who spends her nights in laying traps for innocent "Progressives" and her days in leading her victims to the snare, whose every action is full of sinister meaning, to whom intrigue is both meat and drink, in whose "good morning" there is guile, and on whose lips the multiplication table would be full of undiscoverable, but none the less dangerous wickedness'.

For her friends and colleagues, however, for those who had Liberal interests at heart, there was another Miss Orme. To them, she was 'The quick-witted champion, with a convenient appetite for combat, at once capable and ready to be captain or scapegoat. She is the sort of person of whom it is safe to prophesy she will give rise to a myth, though whether a future generation of women Liberals will explain her as a comet or the north wind I dare not conjecture'. The article went on to sketch in a little of Orme's background, and then highlighted her skill as a debater and reinforced her practical nature: 'Rhetoric and fine language are abhorrent to her. The pathos of facts seems to her more effective than that of mere words, and humour a healthier instrument, as a rule, for the handling of an audience than sentiment'.

As for the *British Weekly* writer (who might have been William Robertson Nicoll), his description was quite accurate, but not his prophecy: Orme died over forty years later, when the causes she cared about had changed beyond recognition and long after her moment in the public eye. Many of the people who wrote the first histories of those causes were busy making myths of other leaders, some of whom had indeed regarded her as a malignant schemer. When I first wrote about her myself, I knew only the bare bones of the schism in the Women's Liberal Federation and nothing about Orme's interactions with either her allies or her antagonists.

Still less did I know anything about the private Eliza's personal relationships. The second bit of evidence is a letter, written in 1888 by Orme herself to her young friend Sam Alexander. Very few of her letters have survived—at one time, I thought that nothing like this would ever surface. It still exists because Samuel Alexander (1859–1938) happened to become a distinguished philosopher of Manchester University, where his papers are carefully preserved in an archive. The handlist to the collection is online, which is how Google helped me find a bundle of eighteen letters written to Alexander by Eliza Orme. He was ten years her junior, and a friend (or possibly a relative) of the family of Reina Emily Lawrence. There is a lot of variety in the correspondence—advice about handling a delicate situation; affectionate praise for his first book; counsel about how to draft his will; news about her visits to Ireland on business, first for the Liberals and later for employers. On this particular occasion she refused to take Sam's 'no' for an answer to an invitation to a social gathering in a fashionable London suburb. 'Besides you ought to want to', she wrote. 'It is pleasure of a very high kind to listen to beautiful music and recitations and refined conversation surrounded with pictures and clever Cambridge students with exceedingly classic profiles. And even the eating and drinking will be of an ennobling kind—for bananas are very cultured food and iced lemonade Oscary Wildey'. The teasing, almost giggly, tone of this letter is extraordinary, and such a far cry from both the arch-villain scheming to bring down the Women's Liberal Federation and the quick-witted champion of worthwhile causes. In the context of all the other letters to Alexander, I can confirm that this missive is not at all flirtatious. But it is intimate. And it gives a voice to someone who felt at home among bohemian artists, writers, publishers, and journalists, someone who was not afraid to allude to decadence. We will see that she lived among people like that too, in the west-London neighbourhood known as Bedford Park. But her work was in Chancery Lane, where the barristers had their chambers.

Both of these illuminating scraps of evidence about Eliza Orme as public politician and private friend came to light only recently with the help of search engines. For most of the last four decades, her life was not much more than a shadowy sketch that did not fit its background.

Readers who want to read the *British Weekly* article and the Alexander letters for themselves will look in vain, at this point, for a footnote to guide their research. Even though the other books and articles I have written are conventionally documented, I came to understand this one would have to be different. There is, of course, a list of sources in an appendix, for those scholars and students who want to pursue Eliza Orme further. But in order for that to happen, I believe my task is to show why this woman was 'hidden from history' for so long and thus restore to her a voice and a face that the women and men of her time might have recognized. It is not a coincidence that so many of her contemporaries have been researched and contextualized, in politics, social reform, literature, and science, while this one's context was legal study and practice where women did not appear. Discovering and interpreting all the biographical and genealogical information, sorting out which contemporary networks she joined and which she evaded, and speculating about what those facts and connections convey—all that research happened over decades, as my own assumptions and judgments changed alongside changing technologies and methodologies.

When I first encountered Miss Orme, all I knew was that she helped George Gissing, the novelist, when he was in a tight spot. Back in those days, the mid-to-late 1980s, I was enrolled in a graduate Victorian Studies program, mostly concerned with British social history but required to take an interdisciplinary seminar and one course on literature. In the latter I learned about Gissing, who was into neither feminist activism nor aestheticism, being the rather unhappy writer of novels like *New Grub Street* and *The Odd Women*. He modelled no characters on Orme. But after he met her through the publisher they shared, he came to depend on her for legal advice and hands-on practical assistance in the breakdown of his second marriage. I was beginning to enjoy research challenges, especially this one after I discovered that Gissing's 'Miss Orme' had the letters LL.B. after her name. There were no search engines in those days, but if a person in the past had published books or journalism to their credit, they had left a trace in card catalogues and periodical indexes that could be pursued on library shelves. Later there would be deeper explorations, in archives and record offices in London. A professor of literature encouraged my efforts, not least because they might offer him ammunition in a scholarly spat with a rival academic interested in the same novelist. For those two men, Eliza Orme was an adjunct to Gissing; and for Gissing himself, she was 'a very strong-minded woman, who has been a good friend to me'. If the novelist knew she was trained in law and prominent in politics, he never mentioned that fact in his letters or diary. In that sense, my Eliza Orme has been the one I rescued from the indignity of being a minor character in someone else's life. But to be fair to Gissing, neither he nor anyone else in the 1890s had a way to think about her education and experience. And to be fair to the Gissing scholars, and to me, in the 1980s we were just beginning to learn how to think about such things ourselves.

1. An Unthinkable Job
for a Woman

The challenge of trying to explain what it meant that women could not be lawyers in Victorian Britain reminds me of a novel I read many years ago. P. D. James's *An Unsuitable Job for a Woman* is about a female private detective, Cordelia Gray, whose professional activities raised eyebrows. But 1972, when that book was set and published, was well into the second wave of the feminist movement in Britain. Eliza Orme lived at the time of the first wave, which extended from the moderate 'suffragist' campaigns of the 1860s to the militant 'suffragettes' of the 1910s. The key issue of those years was to get the law changed to permit women to vote in parliamentary elections on the same basis as men. That generation also sought to create a range of suitable jobs for women—occupational work in shops and offices, professional careers in teaching and medicine, even a few private detectives. Feminists of the 1860s and 70s worked to change the law, around issues like married women's property and appropriate working conditions as well as women's suffrage, but they did not devote their collective energy to breaking into the legal profession. That was beyond unsuitable: it was unthinkable.

Orme has been accorded a modest place in the history of women's professional work in law on the strength of her 1888 degree, the Bachelor of Laws (LL.B.) from University College London, the first ever in England. That was remarkable, but not unthinkable; it was regarded by contemporaries as a notable achievement, but one that had nothing to do with the realities of professional accreditation in a patriarchal society. Indeed, Letitia Walkington earned the same degree at the Royal University of Ireland a few months later. But as women, Letitia and Eliza could no more be full-fledged lawyers than they could be clergy or soldiers or sit on juries, because they were not regarded as equal to

          https://doi.org/10.11647/OBP.0392.01

men. Thirty years went by, encompassing the turn of a new century and a world war, before the Sex Disqualification (Removal) Act of 1919 allowed the first women to qualify as barristers and solicitors. Or to put it another way, Eliza Orme's best years for work and achievement were long behind her before the notion of licensed women practitioners in the legal profession stopped being unthinkable.

I put it that way because, while it is impossible not to say that Orme was the first woman in England to earn a law degree, it is also inherently misleading. She was never allowed to use the academic training of her discipline, the rigorous lectures and examinations in jurisprudence, legal history, political economy and other subjects. Not directly, not to be a barrister or solicitor. And yet she had a life to live and a living to make, both before and after earning that academic qualification. It is even more misleading to assert that she failed to be called to the bar or to join the Law Society. To say that is to fall into what historians call 'presentism', which means projecting contemporary social assumptions backwards onto the past. It is very difficult to think ourselves back to the 1870s (even the 1970s seem impossibly long ago!) to a time when women's full equality meant something, but not what it does now. Then, full equality meant the vote, and protection for married women's property, but almost nobody could imagine a worldview built on assumptions about reliable contraception and socially-sanctioned childcare. It also meant that women should struggle (and it was a struggle) to become doctors, because medicine was a caring profession and there were situations where treatment from someone of the same sex was desirable. None of these visions of equality, however, suggested that women should be licenced to practice law. They did not stretch to a challenge, on the basis of gender, to an enterprise at the heart of cultural, social, economic, and political life, a challenge to that ramshackle non-code of judgments, traditions, assumptions, and interpretations that kept Britain's whole patriarchal machine going. Ladies scarcely belonged in the courtroom as witnesses, most people believed, and certainly not as prosecutors, jurors, or judges. Not when subjects might arise that were deemed inappropriate for ladies to hear, especially unmarried ones. To allow women to be lawyers would have been to upset a whole lot of assumptions better left unquestioned. The prestige of the profession might diminish if women were allowed to participate. And at a more mundane economic level, the innovation would create a body of competent, disciplined competitors for male lawyers in the marketplace. Into this impossible situation, the young Eliza Orme calmly proposed to insert herself.

She might even have had a further goal in mind. Let us consider the way an ambitious young man of the late-Victorian decades prepared himself for a career in public life. Not necessarily, but quite often, he began with a university degree in law. He followed that up with a few years in professional practice while he went about getting acquainted with powerful people by participating in the activities of social clubs, political parties and other special-interest associations. He also, quite often, made a name for himself with occasional journalism, a name that aligned him with the political views of powerful men in the generation ahead of him while drawing their attention to his own attributes. Eliza Orme's university mentors were providing that sort of background to her male peers, and she was smart enough to recognize how the process worked. I do not know her motivations, but having observed that she took each of those career-building steps herself, I am prepared to speculate about where she hoped they would take her.

She prepared herself for public life by getting involved with various liberal causes, notably Home Rule for Ireland, while still a student. Once she had the degree in hand, she began to manage a newspaper for a Liberal Party organization, writing editorials on political subjects and serving on the organization's executive council. But given the time and place she lived in, that organization was a women's auxiliary and the newspaper was their organ. And this is where the story gets complicated. She was solidly committed to women's suffrage, but she was also prepared to strategically compromise that commitment in order not to embarrass the leadership of the Liberal Party. Part of this attitude likely came from her legal training and her pragmatic approach to life. But part of it might also have been ambition. Thwarted ambition, I have to say. She certainly had some successes, but she was not, nor ever could be, a candidate for Member of Parliament, and never elected to a position where she could contribute to changing the government's approach to governing Ireland. That does not mean she did not think about it. Starting out as a teenage activist in the 1860s, she probably expected the vote would come to women in plenty of time for her to use law as a stepping-stone to politics. That had, after all, happened in several other jurisdictions, so why not in Britain?

But before we get to her story, it is time to tell you a bit about mine.

Eliza and Me, and the 1980s

Just before I got acquainted with Eliza Orme and began to learn about how academic feminist historians thought about women and gender, I also got acquainted with a way of thinking called the history of the book. Book history looks at a handful of things that were long taken for granted—what happens in a reader's brain and body while they are immersed in a book; why publishers have more influence on that experience than authors might want to admit; and how a text makes its way around a community of readers in a myriad of material forms. To put it another way (and now I am quoting myself) book history means studying the way people in the past gave material form to knowledge and stories, how they made intangible texts accessible, in the form of tangible objects like books and periodicals, across the barriers created by time and space. My reputation, such as it is, is for book history rather than women's history—just as Orme's was for liberal politics rather than for legal practice. Now she is remembered differently, and maybe I will be too, one day. Looking back, I realize what a long time it took me to learn to be a historian. I am one, but so unconventional that I have spent a good part of my career trying to explain my discipline to my interdisciplinary colleagues, the book historians—while also interpreting book studies for my disciplinary colleagues, the historians.

I came back to studying history in 1981 at the age of thirty-five. In Jessica and Neil, I had a remarkably satisfactory daughter and a profoundly committed life partner. Behind me were a stalled career, a failed first marriage, and an undistinguished BA in history; ahead of me might have been another job, but instead I began to think about returning to school. Without any particular vocation in another direction, it made sense to enrol in some undergraduate History courses at the University of Toronto to refresh my earlier experience. This time around, the whole enterprise of historical thinking was engaging, in particular the course on Victorian Britain. New scholarship in 'history from below' was both intellectually challenging and compelling from the perspective of social justice. Meanwhile, my tentative start on a career had been in the publishing division of a social service organization promoting justice for people with intellectual disabilities. This was not a literary publisher, but they produced books and a magazine to advance the cause. There

I had learned a bit about how books and journals were put together, and about how a voluntary society interacted with its own publishing program.

One day in the summer of 1982, Neil came home from one of his bookstore prowls with a newsstand copy of the journal *Daedalus*. It had an article that he thought might interest me: 'What is the History of Books?' by Robert Darnton. I had never heard of Darnton, but his historical approach struck a deep chord: a way of thinking about the past that hooked on to my recent experience of book-making. For the information of book historians who are reading this, I still possess that single issue of the journal, complete with a price sticker from Lichtman's bookshop in Toronto. For the information of those who are not book historians, Darnton's article is iconic; it is still read and taught extensively, reprinted and excerpted often, and quoted in almost every introductory essay on the subject. This item, the first material iteration of a much-cited piece of writing, now in the possession of a practitioner in the field, encapsulates almost everything you need to know about book history. It is also almost, but not quite, the last you will hear about book history in these pages.

By the time I read the article, I was preparing to begin a master's degree at York University. In those days, York and the University of Toronto sponsored a joint Victorian Studies MA program. This entailed an interdisciplinary seminar on literature and history, and the requirement to take one full course in the discipline outside one's specialty. The seminar was initially terrifying, but I quickly made friends with a couple of women who were fellow students. There were two professors, a historian, Albert Tucker from York, and a literary scholar, John M. (Jack) Robson from Toronto. The seminar met on the U. of T. campus, in the very room at Victoria College where Robson led the project to edit the complete works of John Stuart Mill. We all brought our own undergraduate backgrounds and graduate ambitions to a set of readings that included both novels and histories. I was even more nervous about the second obligation, not having any experience with studying English literature since those long-ago undergraduate days. One offering, from Michael Collie, seemed especially daunting, with a syllabus full of books I had never heard of and some not even by literary authors. Another looked safer, covering Dickens and Gaskell and Brontë: but that one was fully subscribed. I was signed in, perforce, to Collie's course, and entered the room with great trepidation. That was not only where I met Eliza Orme, but also where I first found people to talk to about the history of the book.

Later, we joked that this was a course on Victorian authors named George: Borrow, Eliot, Gissing, and Meredith. My first essay was about George Eliot's relationship with her publishers, but Gissing was inescapable. Michael Collie had recently compiled a bibliography of the novelist's writings and was deeply enmeshed in the minutiae of that troubled life. He was also engaged in a rivalry with the preeminent Gissing scholar, based in France, Pierre Coustillas: they disagreed on almost everything and reviewed each other's books scathingly. Gissing had needed a lot of help in the 1890s, not least to extricate himself from an unfortunate marriage. One of the women who provided aid and comfort was called Eliza Orme. The following year, I undertook to write a paper about her. Coustillas, in his edition of the novelist's diary, had said she was kind to Gissing. Collie, perhaps only to be contrarian, suggested there might be more to her life than niceness. I went to the *National Union Catalogue* to see what books, if any, this paragon might have written. She had two, and her name was inscribed thus: Eliza Orme, LL.B. I asked Michael what he thought that meant, and he was unimpressed: 'maybe an honorary degree?' he speculated. That did not sit well with my feminist sensibilities, and it served as a research challenge.

It is difficult now, in 2024, to reconstruct how, in 1984, I went about finding out who Eliza Orme was. I have forgotten a lot, and research methods have changed so much. For that first assignment I had only York University's Scott Library, and the occasional foray to Robarts Library at the University of Toronto, at my disposal. (And sadly I no longer possess the essay I wrote.) There was no internet, no search engine, just print catalogues and print indexes in the reference section of the libraries, and access to Inter-Library Loan for really obscure works. I suppose I asked them to borrow copies of her books, *Lady Fry of Darlington* and *The Life of Saram Chana Pal*, from other institutions. Probably the resources like *Poole's Index to Periodical Literature* and the *Reader's Guide to Periodical Literature* turned up one or two of her articles in mainstream journals like *The Examiner* and *Longman's Magazine*. With an index reference in hand, I could find the relevant issues on the library shelves. (The fifth volume of the *Wellesley Index to Victorian Periodicals*, with its crucial index to authors, didn't appear until several years later.) There wasn't much information, but the fragments were intriguing. Moreover, they didn't jigsaw together into a coherent narrative, which is perhaps why they were unsettling and ultimately unforgettable. She had written some sort of a government report, too (although I don't think I found that until later). I itched to know more. But the English course was just a course, Victorian Studies was not a viable program for a doctorate, certainly not for a historian. Anyway, nobody in the History department was open to supervising a PhD on women in nineteenth-century Britain and why they were not allowed to be lawyers. Even in the mid-eighties, such a program of study was still pretty close to unthinkable.

As I have mentioned, John M. Robson was a leading expert on John Stuart Mill and almost from the beginning I knew that Orme knew Mill. However it never occurred to me to consult Jack about my Eliza Orme research. Had I done so, the trajectory of the project might have been very different. But despite the ideal of a Victorian Studies program integrating history and literature, the academic world operates in remarkably water-tight compartments. Jack was a wonderful mentor to me, taking an interest in my dissertation work as it evolved, and giving me opportunities to take on some academic leadership, but we never discussed this mutual interest. I also got to know his wife Ann Robson, whose research as a historian focused on Mill's step-daughter Helen Taylor. It was not until years later that I learned Ann Robson had written a very brief article about some editorial work that Orme did for Taylor, and decades after that when the internet helped me find Mill scheming to give Eliza Orme her own opportunities in women's movement leadership. But this is to get ahead of the story.

It was another of the Georges—not Gissing but George Borrow, the author of a Victorian best-seller in 1843 called *The Bible in Spain*—who helped me find a research program for a PhD. Michael Collie had spent time the previous summer in the archives of the British and Foreign Bible Society, in whose employ Borrow had found the source material for what we might now call a work of creative non-fiction but is conventionally regarded as a travel book. When I told Michael I thought I would like to do something on the history of publishing, he told me that the Bible Society still had all its nineteenth-century publishing records. To a historian, the fact that the publishing in question did not pertain to works of literature was irrelevant. What was important was that the Society worked with printers and binders to transform the technology of book production, and that I could identify the people involved, the women as well as the men, and the way the society played gender off against religion, and vice versa. My official advisor, Albert Tucker, was most impressed by the existence of the archive; he did not think of the project as book history, but rather as social history. Michael understood, though, and became my unofficial advisor. I kept in touch with Michael and his other students as we all embarked together on learning about a new way to think about the book. Together we read *Bibliography and the Sociology of Texts*, a radical approach to the study of the material book by a literary scholar called D. F. McKenzie. Darnton and McKenzie, between them, provided the intellectual scaffolding for the dissertation that became my first book, *Cheap Bibles*, and for most of the scholarship that came later. The PhD was 1989, the book came out in 1991, I started my first academic appointment, at the University of Windsor in 1993 and was tenured in 1998.

By the time I finished the doctorate, the study of women's history was much more established than it had been when I started, and so was the history of the book. It is difficult now, in the 2020s, to describe what studies in both social history and book history were like in the 1980s. Both were hovering on the verge of radical transformation, but there was very little academic infrastructure to support the intellectual excitement. Of course, there were precursors of various kinds, especially in the study of Victorian fiction and poetry by women. In departments of history, however, people like Leonore Davidoff and Catherine Hall on the gender side, and people like Darnton on the books side, were just beginning to supervise their own graduate students. There was no one like them in Toronto, not for modern British history, and I was not in a position to move. Had there been a potential advisor and mentor in women's history, my choices might have been different. We women students did some reading on our own, but the official coursework requirements were focused on issues of social class, not gender. There was no historian who specialized in book history, either, but Collie was a bibliographer and he introduced me to the other bibliographers who worked in English departments and university libraries in the city. Bibliography was yet another field that was transforming in the eighties, at that time just on the verge of its encounter with social and cultural history—D. F. McKenzie meeting Robert Darnton.

Even before my dissertation was finished and ready to defend, I started applying for appointments in modern British history in universities—mostly in Canada, but a few in the United States, too. There were not many available. For people on the job market in my discipline, the pattern has been to mark time while enriching one's research portfolio by securing a postdoctoral fellowship. A postdoc also provides a modest income. My first application for a fellowship, in 1989, was unsuccessful; my second, in 1990, was successful. The first would have been in women's history, a project on Eliza Orme and other women seeking to be lawyers in Victorian Britain. My article on Orme had been published in *Atlantis* (a Canadian women's studies journal) the same year, and a professor at Carleton University, Deborah Gorham, was keen to supervise the postdoc. But the application was not funded and there was no explanation why not. My second attempt was in book history, a project on the archives of the publishers Henry S. King and Charles Kegan Paul (archives that were conveniently available on microfilm). The King/Paul research led to my second book, and it promised to contribute to a third, the product of an ongoing collaboration with Michael Collie in the form of a study of the International Scientific Series. King and Paul had been the British publishers of that series. But do not look for that book in the library; the collaboration ended abruptly before our work together was finished.

The *Atlantis* piece was called 'Sound-Minded Women: Eliza Orme and the Study and Practice of Law in Late-Victorian England'. Before being accepted by *Atlantis*, the article was turned down by *Victorian Studies* and by *Albion*, the two leading journals of the time. (I still have the reports, which can be summed up as the reviewers telling me Orme really was not all that important.) The quote in my title came from one of her own articles, published in *The Examiner* in 1874:

> We have often felt the want of a word to express the opposite of a weak-minded woman. 'Strong-minded' unfortunately suggests a host of weaknesses of which a very typical one is that peculiar taste which a few women have for trying to dress like men. The women who have been

driven into notoriety by the refusal of just and moderate recognition, and those who try to enliven the dulness of a purposeless life by being uselessly eccentric, are generally called strong-minded. Society has adopted the word to describe the abnormal result of its own over-restrictions. How, then, can we speak of women who can take a journey by railway without an escort, who can stand by a friend through a surgical operation, and who yet wear ordinary bonnets and carry medium-sized umbrellas? The *Saturday Review* gives us exactly the right expression when it speaks of 'sound-minded women'. The word explains itself.

Obliquely, too, Eliza Orme's jibe at the social restrictions on independent-minded middle-class women seeking a just and moderate recognition also explained itself.

At the time I characterized Orme as 'a prominent public figure and a prosperous spinster'. I had not found any personal papers, just some census records and entries in city directories along with a handful of references in books and periodicals about better-known contemporaries. Anxious for something of human interest to recount, I cited the intriguing possibility that George Bernard Shaw might have used Orme as a model when he created the character of Vivie Warren, the independent professional daughter in *Mrs Warren's Profession*. Even better, I mentioned how George Gissing noted that she smoked a cigar with the gentlemen, 'as a matter of course', after a dinner-party. I had access to an interview she had given to the *Law Journal* in 1903 when she was fifty-five years old, to her journalism in mainstream periodicals, and other miscellaneous evidence, some of it collected in odd moments during my dissertation research in British libraries. With this I wove together a narrative and concluded that 'Eliza Orme would be dismayed to know that she was being represented to posterity in terms of her gender. She thought of herself as an educated person, an authoritative expert, prepared to give her opinion on subjects ranging from Home Rule in Ireland to jurisprudence in India. Even her views on women's work and education were offered as if from a distance, as if the restrictions of contemporary society did not apply to Eliza Orme'. All these years later, I suppose I would still say most of that, though I hope I have found a better historical framework to express the ideas. Finally, though, I do have something more personal to report than about that cigar. Still, the anecdote did make a difference back then. One colleague had got hold of her views on the working conditions for barmaids and drew the conclusion that she must be teetotal: the episode of her smoking a cigar with a party of men was enough to convince him that he was wrong.

Another scholar read that article too, someone who had heard of my work on Eliza Orme and tried to make contact, initially through Michael Collie. Incredibly, she was right there on the York University campus, but not in the History Department, nor in the English Department, or anywhere in the faculty of arts or humanities—she was in the Osgoode Hall Law School. Which, as far as us getting together intellectually was concerned, might as well have been on the other side of the moon. Mary Jane Mossman's book, *The First Women Lawyers: A Comparative Study of Gender, Law and the Legal Professions* (2006) had a whole chapter on Eliza Orme that leaned heavily on my 1989 article, citing it generously. But we only met much later and have since made up for lost time by becoming very good friends.

I did not really feel like a historian while doing a PhD in the subject at York University—that came later, thanks to my colleagues at the University of Windsor—but I did feel like a researcher. I discovered a passion for the archives, and a capacity to spend patient hours reading through documents written in the nineteenth century. Some of them in atrocious handwriting, though thankfully not all. The French historian Le Roy Ladurie said that historians are either truffle hunters (who search for nuggets of knowledge) or parachutists (who survey the past from a great height). I learned at York that I am the first kind of historian. A fellow student who was a parachutist—someone immersed in theoretical approaches—was rather disdainful. She waited to go to the archives until after she had worked out what questions she hoped to find answered there. Whereas I went to the archives early, eagerly, even joyfully—just to find out what was there and to display it to my readers. The comparison is too clumsy, really. All of us are both kinds of historian. But my way of approaching the Bible Society of the first half of the nineteenth century allowed me to see something that had been overlooked by other scholars, which was that they were a publisher, and not really a religious organization. (It helped that I already knew about publishing by an advocacy organization in my own time.) All that research also prepared me for a decades-long search for nuggets of information about Eliza Orme, beginning with her life before law.

2. Before Law, 1848 to 1871

Eliza Orme was born into a family whose members were principled about the wise use of their wealth and privilege. The Ormes were vigorous people who appreciated artistic beauty and good design. They cultivated relationships with some of the leading painters, poets, intellectuals, and illustrators of the period. The father was a successful businessman in the liquor trade. Their London home was on Avenue Road, near Regent's Park and his distillery was in Blackfriars, on the Thames River near St Paul's Cathedral. Oddly enough, we know more about the mother than the father in this family, because the elder Eliza Orme brought a network of high-powered literary and political connections to her marriage, whereas Charles Orme's interests can only be guessed at through the sort of people he entertained and the support he must have given to his wife's political and cultural interests. ('Must have given', because the stereotypical nineteenth-century paterfamilias could and often did shut such interests down. But not this one.)

What follows is the result of hundreds of hours of research, none of it straightforward, much of it a matter of fruitless scrambles down rabbit holes, and a lot of it gleaned from scrutinizing census records that have only become available quite recently. All the relevant people's names, along with birth and death dates and family connections, are listed in the 'Major Figures, and Families' section of the Appendix to this volume.

Eliza Andrews, known as 'Mrs Charles Orme' after her marriage (but I call her Eliza Orme senior) was the daughter of an intellectual clergyman. The Rev. Edward Andrews tutored John Ruskin as that young man prepared to become the polymath critic who dominated the intellectual and artistic worlds of the late nineteenth century. To his credit, the Rev. Mr. Andrews tutored his own daughters too,

 https://doi.org/10.11647/OBP.0392.02

in Greek, Latin, and French. In fact, some of these girls have been credited with introducing Ruskin to the Pre-Raphaelite artists he later championed. Two more of the Andrews sisters married two brothers: Emily, the famous poet Coventry Patmore (which makes Emily the model for the original 'angel in the house' of her husband's poem and of Victorian mythology), and Georgina, George Morgan Patmore. Georgina's husband died in 1856, and she became a member of the Orme household. Whatever Coventry Patmore may have anticipated, this family rejected his poem's vision of cloistered domestic femininity. Flora Masson (Eliza senior's granddaughter and Georgina's great-niece) wrote that 'Among the friends who used to gather in the Avenue Road garden on summer evenings, or round the hospitable dinner-table, were the Tennyson family, the Rossetti family, and the two Pre-Raphaelites, Thomas Woolner and Holman Hunt'. Let me decode that for you: Flora was dropping several of the most distinguished names of the time, older ones like Tennyson in the same breath with some of the latest avant-garde artists.

Eliza Orme senior quickly became a sort of patron of the arts, and especially of the group who called themselves the Pre-Raphaelite Brotherhood. Because of that, I have been able to trace some descriptions of her appearance and personality, and also some references to objects associated with both her and them. The artist John Brett made the charcoal drawing that is probably her portrait (see Fig. 1). Brett described Mrs Orme as 'highly intellectual, cultivated and fascinating.' The writer William Rossetti described her as a 'lady ... of rich physique, with luminous dark eyes.' William's brother, the poet-illustrator Dante Gabriel Rossetti, noted that he and William and their sister Christina had spent several evenings with the Ormes, 'and indeed, I think we may now consider ourselves in the circle of family friends'. Dante Gabriel Rossetti drew a sketch of the sculptor Thomas Woolner and gave it to the senior Eliza Orme because she was Woolner's friend and patron. This sketch portrait remained in the family for decades and is now in the collections of the National Portrait Gallery. Woolner himself made and gave to her a medallion of Tennyson; he also made medallions of the mother and two of her daughters, Rosaline and Helen.

Fig. 1 Portrait of a woman, possibly Eliza Orme senior (1854–55, John Brett), ©The British Museum.

Rosaline Orme married David Masson, a rather glamorous, up-and-coming young man who brought a more intellectual and political kind of modernity into this artistic household. He was one of the first scholars of English literature (which, believe it or not, was new as a university subject in those days). He was a well-connected editor and journalist as well as an academic. Through Masson the family got to know John Stuart Mill, who later became an important influence on the younger Eliza's political and professional choices. Thomas Carlyle, Douglas Jerrold, W. M. Thackeray, and Giuseppe Mazzini visited too, along with the Pre-Raphaelite artists already mentioned, and a host of lesser-known figures. The Massons' first two children were born at the Regent's Park house. Even after they moved to Scotland, for David to take up the Chair of English Literature at Edinburgh University, the family spent a month every year with their London family, and the London relatives also went north to reciprocate the visit. A few years later another Orme daughter, Julia, repeated her sister's pattern when she married the physician and scientist Henry Charlton Bastian and remained in her parents' home with her professional-man husband and growing family.

The influence of these two live-in brothers-in-law on the young Eliza Orme may have been profound, but this is something I have to speculate about, piecing together the evidence that exists and probing the silences. In Masson's case it seems to have been the people he knew and perhaps his worldly demeanour, rather than his specific subject, English literature. Whereas Bastian was a physician specializing in neurology and psychology; and Eliza went on to study physics and chemistry at university, and later taught chemistry to school children. Two of her brothers were also doctors, so it is quite plausible that either they or Bastian influenced her initial decision to study science, perhaps intending to go into medicine. What we do not know is why she changed her mind and turned to law (although I have my own ideas about that). Meanwhile we do know about the influence of her mother. The elder Eliza Orme was active in the early days of the women's suffrage movement, signing petitions and attending meetings—and sometimes taking her daughter along.

They do not seem to have been an especially religious family. The only evidence I have found on that score is the census records, which indicate that several of the children were christened at Calvinist independent chapels. But with distilled spirits as the foundation of the family's fortunes, and such a disparate, cultured, and sophisticated circle of friends, they do not seem to have been particularly puritanical. Nor, as far as I know, were they pillars of the Church of England.

I write in more detail about each of Eliza's parents and siblings in Chapter 4, but for now let us take a snapshot of the family in 1861, when the census generated its record of a household of seventeen people including twelve-year-old Eliza. Both parents were in their prime: Charles Orme was fifty-four years of age and the elder Eliza was forty-five. All their children were still at home. The eldest, Charles Edward Orme, was a surgeon and unmarried at twenty-seven. Rosaline Masson was twenty-five (David was thirty-eight, and their children Flora and David Orme Masson were five and three). Next in line should have been Helen Foster Orme, who would have been twenty-four, but she had died in 1857. Julia Orme (later Bastian) was twenty-one; her brother Campbell was eighteen. The three youngest sisters were Blanche, Eliza, and Beatrice at sixteen, twelve, and three years old respectively. Georgina Patmore was thirty-four. There were four servants in residence, who must have kept extremely busy taking care of this multigenerational family.

What was Eliza Orme doing and thinking in 1861, at twelve years of age? We know very little and have to speculate (responsibly) and imagine (intuitively) the rest. We do know that she and Rosaline and one other sister attended Bedford College for Women, though not exactly when. It was one of the first two secondary schools for girls in England. This already set them apart from most other girls of their class, but what made Eliza begin to think about pushing the limits of what women could do? Perhaps there were inspirational teachers whose influence has gone unrecorded. But I also wonder what her mother, her aunts Georgina and Emily and her father's sisters Caroline and Emily Orme, had to say about Eliza's ambitions? How much was she troubled by the death of her sister Helen? What were the rivalries and alliances among that large family of siblings and cousins? (The last-born Orme, Beatrice, was younger than the first Masson child, Flora.) Did Eliza enjoy the visits of her parents' and David Masson's worldly friends and colleagues, and listen in to their talk? Did she join in the conversations?

I speculate, and imagine, that there must have been a good deal of support at home for her ambitions. She faced so many obstacles and prejudices during a remarkable career that it is hard to believe such setbacks could have started at home. Especially since there is evidence of strong role models in that home, for intellectual, and even feminist, womanhood. So they were probably supportive when Eliza, at nineteen, decided to be among the first women in England to study at a university. Some of those institutions, under pressure, had begun cautiously to allow this innovation, although they generally postponed the awarding of actual degrees to women until decades later. In May of 1869 the University of London set its first examination for women students to qualify. Eliza Orme was one of nine women (later remembered as 'the London nine') who wrote that rigorous exam, and one of the six who passed it. Around the same time, though, she also applied to be a member of the initial class at Girton College, Cambridge, aiming to take French, Mathematics and Chemistry while politely declining studies in Scripture. So she was still considering her options. We know that she did go to University College London in 1872, first studying the sciences and later switching to law; we do not know why she chose London over Cambridge. It would have been more difficult to pursue a legal education at Cambridge, but she did not decide upon the law until after a couple of years of study.

Those years of the late 1860s and early 1870s were exhilarating ones for people with progressive ideas, about politics, about law, about women's rights. John Stuart Mill's *The Subjection of Women* was published in 1869. Sheldon Amos, writing anonymously in the *Westminster Review*, opined that 'With the appearance of this work, we trust the old era of female subordination has finally passed away' and in the next paragraph went on to comment favourably on a new edition of Barbara Bodichon's *Brief Summary in Plain Language of the most important Laws of England concerning Women*. The Orme family not only knew Mill and Amos, they knew Bodichon, too, and both the elder and the younger Eliza Orme were connected to the movement centred in Langham Place of which Bodichon was a leader. In Chapter 3 of this book, I speculate that the seeds of Eliza Orme's commitment to the study and practice of law might even have planted by Barbara Leigh Smith Bodichon.

As the next census came around, when Eliza Orme was twenty-two in 1871, most of the rest of the family were still at home, but she was away at work, teaching chemistry in Lydia Millicent, a village near Swindon in Wiltshire. Along with a companion (or perhaps it was more of a chaperone), she lived in the home of a retired barrister and his wife, Joseph and Mary A. Snowe. The person described as 'companion of a lady' was Jane G. Scales and apart from young Eliza there seems to have been no other 'lady' in the household requiring companionship or a chaperone. I have not yet been able to identify any more connections among these people than the census record, nor any information as to why Eliza Orme travelled from London to Wiltshire for work. Perhaps there was an advertisement and she merely applied, or perhaps someone in her vast family network facilitated the arrangement. A few years later, Frances Buss, one of the pioneers of girls' education, was counting on help with science classes at the Camden School for Girls from Miss Orme and a Mr Aveling. Perhaps Miss Buss knew something it took me a long time to find out: that Eliza Orme had already had experience as a teacher of science.

I want to pause for a moment over this path Orme did not take, towards a career in the hard sciences: chemistry or physics or mathematics. Having passed the University of London's rigorous Special Examination in 1869, she wrote another examination for women in 1870, this time for a Special Certificate in Physics and Chemistry. The latter, presumably, qualified her for the teaching job in Wiltshire. When she began to consider moving to the study of law in December 1872, just before her twenty-fourth birthday, she was still intending to take similar certificates in three subjects the following spring: Mathematics, Mechanics, and Political Economy. Certificates like that were hardly the equivalent of the formal degrees that women were still denied, but they were useful preparation and credentials for teaching and might lay the groundwork for later work or further study.

If this book were a novel, the main character's decision to move from the hard sciences to the study of law might be a turning point, and some compelling reason for it would be expounded and justified. As it is, we have to speculate. Perhaps, least original but still plausible, someone might advance the theory of a love affair that ended badly. Or perhaps Eliza had been encouraged towards medicine, by parents or brothers-in-law or other family members, but came independently to a new ambition while away from home. She may have shaken off the influence of a mentor, some man of science whose influence waned as she grew more confident and mature, or as she got to know him better. Was her Wiltshire host Joseph Snowe's practice of law an influence? Or did she face there the realization that teaching was not her métier, though for a woman it was inevitable as the foundation for a career in science? This is not a novel, and we do not know why Eliza Orme forsook mathematics and science for law, only that she did so.

If this were a conventional work of history or biography, the lack of hard evidence about Orme's apparent interest in science, mathematics, and/or logic would make it difficult to incorporate those subjects in the narrative. Knowing the end of the story, too, the plot seems to arc already towards the law and public service and beyond. What I am trying to do here is to leave the possibilities open, and to exercise a bit of imagination. For all I know, she wanted to be an artist, or a creative writer, or even a wife and mother ... or an engineer. There is so little evidence for anything, it is dangerous to put too much emphasis on what is there. If she had not happened to be living in the Snowe household on census day in 1871, my story would be different.

In any case, within a few months of the census-taking, Eliza Orme reappeared in London, and a year later she was a university student. There were formidable advisors available to her at University College.

Those professors who were open to working with women students must have recognized her intelligence and ambition, and some of them may have known her family. The three mentors I am aware of were John Elliott Cairnes and Leonard Courtney, both political economists, and William Alexander Hunter, a barrister-politician. She was in the first mixed-sex class in political economy at University College, taught by Cairnes. He was a highly respected scholar who, with his wife Eliza Cairnes, later facilitated Eliza Orme's approach to Helen Taylor about studying law with a view to practice. Orme mentioned Courtney years later during an interview with the *Law Journal*, and he was possibly influential in her achieving a coveted appointment in 1892. As for Hunter, Orme acknowledged his influence on her study of both Roman law and jurisprudence when she wrote an entry on his life for the *Dictionary of National Biography*. He and she were both on the executive committee of an Association to Promote Women's Knowledge of the Law (around 1878), and much later Hunter was editor of a weekly newspaper to which she contributed leading articles. While there must undoubtedly have been professors who undermined Orme's confidence and impeded her academic progress, these three recognized and supported her ambitions.

When I first started to construct the narrative of Eliza Orme's life in her early twenties, I imagined her as a full-time student at University College, plunging joyfully into learning about law and political economy. But it was not so simple. She had already been forced into an awkward position. As I learned when I consulted the complete works of John Stuart Mill, her name was put forward, by Mill and a colleague, to take leadership in feminist politics. This happened at a time when she was still very young, and when the invitation came at the suggestion of a powerful and highly respected man. Even now, that kind of invitation is difficult to decline, and for an ambitious person in 1871, presumably impossible. As I see it now, she must have looked like what people call 'a safe pair of hands' who would be sensible, pragmatic, and (most importantly) deferential to those to whom she owed her position.

Here is what happened. (And the level of masculine condescension involved is eye-watering!) There was a nasty split in the still-very-new women's suffrage movement, between the London Committee for Women's Suffrage and a group in Manchester. The London leadership included Helen Taylor, stepdaughter to Mill, and a young woman called Caroline Ashurst Biggs. The Manchester leadership were proposing to link the women's suffrage movement with a different, and very controversial, feminist campaign—for the repeal of the Contagious Diseases Acts. Biggs agreed with the Manchester group, while Mill and Taylor wanted to insulate the suffrage movement from the inevitable charges of impropriety that would be associated with a campaign concerned with human sexuality. Mill wrote to a male ally of the movement, proposing that Eliza Orme should replace the unreliable Miss Biggs as the London Committee Secretary. He told his friend: 'I repeat that you need have no fear of Miss Orme not being able to do the work. She would very quickly learn all that is really necessary, and we may hope would be free from that feverish bustle which has made what work has been done seem twice as laborious as it really need be'. Miss Biggs apparently was 'far from judicious' and must have seemed over-endowed with 'feverish bustle', as indeed Mill regarded the people in Manchester collectively.

Fig. 2 John Stuart Mill and Helen Taylor (n.d., photographer unknown), Wikimedia, https://commons.wikimedia.org/wiki/File:J_S_Mill_and_H_Taylor.jpg, CC-PD-Mark.

Thus it was that when Eliza Orme eventually took on positions of leadership in both the women's movement and the Liberal Party, she had behind her the awkward experience of having been parachuted into a job in order to suit someone else's agenda. In some ways, no doubt, it was beneficial. But my hunch is that in 1871, at twenty-two, the appointment as Secretary was too much, too soon, and the resulting challenges may have influenced some of the decisions she made later. At a practical level, she took advantage of the relationship with Taylor and Mill when the time came to make her move to embark on the study of law. Nevertheless, it is important to recognize that when those two powerful, celebrated, feminists put her in charge, they were not working in the best interests of Eliza Orme, but in their own.

Later, when we see how Orme's life ended up, we might identify this moment as a liminal, or perhaps transitional, point in her experience, putting her on the way to becoming a leader either in the women's movement or in the Liberal Party, though perhaps not both. (And in the end, as it happened, neither.) Only after the events of a full long life are known is it possible to recognize where the unalterable choices were made, and which accidents of fate turned out to make a difference. In my own career, the research that forms the backbone of this book was to all intents and purposes abandoned for several decades.

Eliza and Me, 1989–2016

With one important exception, my initial period of intense interest in Eliza Orme ended about 1989, when my postdoctoral fellowship application on women lawyers failed and my *Atlantis* article about Orme was published. That article seemed to drop down a hole, as far as any broader interest in Orme was concerned. It was not quoted or cited, and I was never invited to speak on the subject. It was not much more than a line on my *curriculum vitae*, one of several publications to show that I was a productive historian. Orme's part in the history of women and law was not part of my professional discourse, but it simmered away privately, on a scholarly back burner, with one exception. That was generated by the revival of the Victorian *Dictionary of National Biography*, with plans during the early 1990s for significant expansion of the project. As a beginning, the *DNB* editors planned a *Missing Persons* volume, inviting contributions on some of the many individuals who had been left out of the original publication or its series of supplements. (Orme had contributed biographies of her mentor W. A. Hunter and two other men in the 1901 supplement.) I immediately wrote and suggested her as a subject, and my *Atlantis* article turned out useful after all, as academic legitimation for the proposal. The editors accepted, and the essay appeared when the volume came out in 1993.

On a summer research trip to England, maybe about 1995, I visited the Fawcett Library (later the Women's Library) that was then located in the East End of London at London Guildhall University. This was a quick visit in search of Eliza Orme, research sandwiched in between the 'real work' on my Kegan Paul and International Scientific Series projects. I found a few scraps, and that was exciting, but when I got home there was no time to do anything with them and the notes and photocopies began to fade, untouched. The same went for the letters between Orme and Helen Taylor, which later became so useful. Those were lodged at the London School of Economics, in their British Library of Political and Economic Science. I did get to sit there, just for a day, as far back as the summer of 1990, and transcribe some of the letters—until my time ran out—and vowed to myself that I would go back and finish the job, and then find a way to use them. Some day. That time finally came in 2021, after I had returned to finish the transcription and use it in my chapter about Orme in the edited volume *Precarious Professionals*. But for a long time, those pencilled notes sat fading and abandoned in a file folder.

When I secured a limited-term appointment at the University of Windsor in 1993, it was on the strength of my *Cheap Bibles* monograph and my interest in social and cultural history, including the history of the book. During those first five Windsor years, until 1998, I had the postdoctoral research on the Kegan Paul firms to finish and publish, the planned collaboration on the International Scientific Series to pursue, and the initial stirrings of ideas about applying the ideas of book history to history books. But primarily, for those five years, I was focused on the job market and my academic future—not only applications for appointments elsewhere, but a feverish preoccupation with the possibility that my limited-term appointment at Windsor might be converted to one with tenure. There were, in those days, a few competitions every year where universities advertised for expertise in modern British history. People in my cohort thought the market was terribly tight, and we scrambled for every possibility. (Now in the 2020s the contest has become unimaginably tougher, with many highly trained and qualified applicants vying for only a scant handful of positions.) I discovered to my chagrin that it had not been a good career move to declare myself a book historian. The field was still too new to be recognized by many historians, and its interdisciplinarity was suspect. (I was asked 'Why not go to English?' while a colleague with similar interests whose PhD was in English was told that he should take his application to History.) Even *Cheap Bibles* did not mean much to historians. It was in a Cambridge University Press series on Printing and Publishing History, and book history was not yet mainstream. I applied for everything that looked reasonable and a few things that did not. I travelled two or three times to the annual conference of the American Historical Association, where preliminary interviews were held. I applied to positions at the University of British Columbia and the University of Toronto, and others I can no longer remember. Most of these were the coveted tenure-track posts; a few were for limited-term appointments. If I never got hired, I was going to be in the precarious position of an 'independent scholar' without an institutional base of support. And I did not even get an interview. In the midst of applying for jobs and writing chapters on London publishers, there was not much time to spare for a woman whose position, a century earlier, had been so much more precarious then than mine was now.

When the University of Windsor hired me that first time, in the summer of 1993, it was initially for a two-year limited-term appointment, to teach Modern British History and the European survey course. I rented an apartment in Windsor, but home and family were still a four-hour journey away in Toronto. The appointment existed because its incumbent had become Dean, but there was no immediate institutional appetite for making it permanent for me. So Neil stayed with his civil service job in Toronto; Jessica was at McGill doing her undergraduate degree; we were together at weekends and holidays. This new life was a bit complicated, but also liberating and exciting. After two years, I had a respected place in the department and most students seemed to like me well enough. Being at a university gave me a good base to apply for research fellowships and conference panels. It was in these years that SHARP was founded (the Society for the History of Authorship,

Reading, and Publishing) and I attended its first meetings in New York (1993), Washington DC (1994) and Edinburgh (1995) and joined its Board of Directors in 1997. I went to Ireland for the first time, for a bit of Kegan Paul research, and fitted holidays in among the visits to libraries.

The best thing about arriving at Windsor, though, was that I became fully a historian, in a way I never quite had as a graduate student or postdoctoral fellow, oriented as I had been to the interdisciplinarity of book history. My Windsor colleagues (at least those of my own academic generation) were thrilled to have an active and ambitious scholar in their ranks, someone interested in sharing new approaches to cultural history, to women's history. At the same time, though, they were tenured and I was not even tenure-track. It was through our shared enthusiasm for what we all meant by 'history' and our ambitions for teaching and research (and counterposed by the simultaneous lack of enthusiasm for my c.v. on the part of hiring committees) that I began to understand the position of our discipline within book history. (Briefly: in book history, historians are intellectually central but numerically subordinate, outnumbered by literary scholars and librarians.) So the experience of academic precarity, including its partial alleviation, became part of my intellectual development and eventually helped me understand Eliza Orme's precarious position with respect to the practice of law. For both of us, being competent, intelligent, and energetic was not enough in the face of an implacable system. As it happened, I was the best-published and most active scholar in my department, but this did nothing to change the fact that my appointment came to an end in 1995 and I had to compete and interview to be rehired for a further limited term. And again in 1997. However, that cycle could not go on for ever. The collective agreement between the University and its Faculty Association stipulated that limited terms could not extend past five years, and the provost still showed no interest in creating a tenure-track appointment in its place. My local colleagues liked my work, but the system was structured in such a way that they were powerless, as I was, to change the situation.

The story of my precarity had a happy ending, although it came with a painful twist that made job security difficult to celebrate. The University kept me on tenterhooks until the very end. By the summer of 1998, even if they had advertised a further Limited Term appointment, I would not have been eligible, because I had been employed on those terms for a full five years. From Windsor's point of view, it was going to be either a new LTA or (if the provost would approve) a tenure-track appointment. From mine, it was either the latter or nothing. There were a few weeks of optimism, then the news that the provost had decided against awarding the appointment to History. Desolation: tears in my office, crying on the shoulder of my friend who was the department head and later at home on Neil's. And then, a miraculous change of heart. The tenure-stream line was opened, I applied, interviewed once again, was hired and duly tenured. But job security did not guarantee a straightforward research agenda because, within a few months, there was another debacle. My collaboration with Michael Collie broke down and we decided to go our separate ways with what had been a joint project. It took me a while to realize how significant was 1998: in that year, my career became secure and I untied myself from the intellectual apron-strings of a mentor.

However reluctantly tenure was granted, both its security and intellectual independence had beneficial effects on my confidence and my fortunes. Perhaps the first international recognition was the invitation to become a Trustee of the Cambridge Project for the Book, and the second was to be General Editor of a series on book history for the University of Toronto Press. I also got hold of the idea of putting my two research specialties together and studying the publishing history of history books. That led to a research grant, and later another one. I had my first sabbatical in 2000 and presented some ideas about the essential interdisciplinarity of book history at the SHARP conference in Mainz that year. There was vague talk of a collection of essays on various disciplinary approaches to be published by the U. of T. Press, of which my contribution would be a chapter. The vague talk went on for a good few years, and eventually the project was abandoned. I proposed to the Press that instead I expand my own chapter, and my own ideas, to make a little book that would stand alone. This was published in 2006, *Old Books & New Histories*, and it is still widely read and has been translated. It is the best-known of any of my academic work. That very same year—I was reading proofs for *OBNH* in Oxford—I was accorded the tremendous honour of the Lyell Readership in Bibliography at the University of Oxford. This meant presenting a series of five lectures (eventually five chapters of my next book, *Past into Print*, on the publishing of history in Britain) over a period of two-and-a-half weeks at the Examination Schools. Not to mention being fêted at a reception in the Divinity School, the magnificent medieval building attached to the Bodleian Library. That was all tremendously thrilling, although it had also been pretty stressful, not only in 2006 but for two or three years leading up to the moment.

Something else happened in 2006, and I missed it. Mary Jane Mossman's book, *The First Women Lawyers: A Comparative Study of Gender, Law and the Legal Professions*, came out. With a whole chapter on Eliza Orme. And I missed it. I had even corresponded with Professor Mossman, who was in the Osgoode Hall Law School of York University where I did my PhD. Looking back, I wonder if I might have evaded the knowledge of that book, perhaps looked away from reviews that might have come across my field of vision. I did keep Eliza Orme in mind, or thought I did. If I were in an academic bookstore like Heffer's in Cambridge or Blackwell's in Oxford—or at a conference publisher's booth—and came across a book about nineteenth-century women, I always checked the index for her name. And I filed away the notes of those references. Speaking at the SHARP conference in 2006 in the Netherlands, I was asked to reflect on a still-very-new phenomenon called Google Books. I used the opportunity to search that database on the terms 'Eliza Orme' and 'Miss Orme' and even discovered something I had not known before. But that was all. For most of my career in Windsor, which lasted from 1993 to 2014, I thought of myself as a book historian. Sometimes I imagined that I might return to Eliza Orme when I had retired.

Neil retired first, at the end of 2008, when he was sixty, but we decided I would stay on at Windsor until mid-2014, when I would be sixty-seven. I loved my work, challenging as it was, and he really did not love his. I might have stayed longer if the university had been able to be flexible about teaching loads and give me more time for research, even at a reduced salary. But that was not possible, and I was ready to leave teaching behind. But not research. Even then, though, I still was not talking about going back to Eliza Orme. I had written *Past into Print* but felt I had more to say; I envisioned writing 'a big book about history books' (as I characterized the project) once I was out of the classroom and Neil and I had moved back in Toronto.

A few things changed my mind about the return to Eliza Orme, and two of them happened at conferences right around my retirement. In 2014 'the Berks' was in Toronto. This was the Berkshire Conference on Women's History. I had attended one while still in graduate school and loved the feminist energy of historians of women all gathered in one place. Once or twice I got together with a colleague to propose a Berks session on 'women and the book' but it was always turned down. So this time I was simply attending, not presenting. I went to a session on the history of women in law and heard a paper by Mary Jane Mossman about her work on the first generation of Ontario women who became lawyers. I introduced myself to her afterwards, and we were both thrilled to meet at last. She told me about a new book on George Gissing with new information on Eliza Orme. And we agreed to meet and talk some more.

Then in 2015, the North American Conference on British Studies was in Little Rock, Arkansas. Someone I knew in England asked me to offer commentary on a session where his students were presenting. Their papers were on 'precarious professionals', women in the nineteenth century who were doing work that required specialized knowledge and expertise, but whose gender precluded them being straightforwardly identified as professional with all that implied. In my comments, I mentioned very briefly that Eliza Orme might qualify for that designation, too. The young women went home to England, put together a plan for an edited book on the topic, and asked me to contribute a chapter. That chapter—eventually published in 2021—marked the beginning of my return to studying Eliza Orme.

One more thing happened to switch my research in the direction of Eliza Orme. In the summer of 2016, a year after we had moved from Windsor to Toronto and begun to settle into retirement, Neil was diagnosed with a very aggressive cancer. He died in September. I abandoned the project I had been working on when he first got sick, but another three years went by, and a global pandemic began, before I started working seriously on Eliza Orme, first producing a chapter and an article, and then this book.

3. The Commitment to Law: 1872 to 1888

I still wonder what circumstances made Eliza Orme decide to become a lawyer, when she might have been a medic or a mathematician. Many people make that career commitment on the basis of family tradition, but neither her father nor any of her brothers and brothers-in-law were lawyers. So perhaps it was her professorial mentors who motivated the decision, men like Leonard Courtney, John Elliott Cairnes, and W. A. Hunter. And maybe those men did inspire her, although I doubt if any of them endorsed her most ambitious hopes and dreams. I think that probably their influence was more at the level of installing liberal—and Liberal—political ideals, and perhaps also the notion of law as a means to an end in public life. Instead I like to think that, before she met any of those eminent gentlemen, the seed of the idea might have been planted by her mother's friend, the feminist leader Barbara Leigh Smith Bodichon. Wealthy and independent, Bodichon was involved in founding the *English Woman's Journal* in 1858 and Girton College, Cambridge in 1869. Her book, *A Brief Summary of the Laws of England concerning Women*, had first come out in 1854 and prompted changes in the Married Women's Property Acts. Eliza was only five years old in 1854, but in 1869 a revised and expanded third edition of the book appeared, one that included information on franchise reform and was widely reviewed and discussed. Eliza was twenty-one that year and considering her options for university-level education. I can imagine some exciting and productive conversations taking place between the three of them: the unconventional, experienced feminist politician, her wealthy and well-connected friend Mrs Charles Orme, and the determined young Eliza. Perhaps that was the moment, as I speculated in Chapter 2, when she moved from an interest in science and mathematics to embrace the study of law.

  https://doi.org/10.11647/OBP.0392.03

Fig. 3   Barbara   Leigh   Smith   Bodichon   (1861,   Samuel   Laurence),
©National Portrait Gallery, London.

Books and movies about the Victorian women's movement mostly focus on the campaign for the vote, and to a lesser extent on the one for respectable opportunities for middle-class women ('ladies') to earn their own livings by work. But what kind of work did they envisage? Leaders in the movement recognized that if a lady were to avoid moving from the financial support of her father to that of a husband (that is, to remain single) she would have to find a job of some sort. If she got married she would have children, which was deemed to preclude work outside the home altogether. Meanwhile, if a woman was of the working class, a whole other set of social and economic conventions applied. The first difficulty was that a 'lady' could not respectably take the kinds of jobs that working-class women did, and the second was that clerical work—otherwise eminently suitable—was restricted to men. At mid-century, a 'lady' could really only work as a governess, because that labour could be carried on under a domestic roof. It was also poorly paid, subject to exploitation, and precarious. The Society for Promoting the Employment of Women existed to remedy this situation. However, in addition to opening up the work of teachers, 'typewriters' (the person, not the technology) and other non-professional occupations, there was a campaign to make it possible for women to be doctors. Medicine was one of three traditional professions; the other two were the law and the clergy, but feminists were not campaigning to enter these. In the case of medicine, reformers like Elizabeth Garrett Anderson and Sophia Jex-Blake were able to argue that women doctors provided an important service to women patients. Whereas the merits of having either legal or theological technicalities explained by women, to women as well as men, remained unthinkable to almost everyone, even feminist leaders.

Such was the situation as Eliza Orme came of age at the end of the 1860s. But that young woman had courage and ambition. Whether or not she shared my opinion that Harriet Taylor and John Stuart Mill took advantage of her goodwill (when they manoeuvred her to fill the secretary's post in the London National Society for Women's Suffrage) she ruthlessly took advantage of her acquaintance with them—and perhaps even their obligation to her—to seek support for an extraordinary project. (And incidentally to announce her resignation from the job they had landed her with a year and a half earlier.) Mill and Taylor were out of London at the time, so she wrote to them. Although Orme had almost certainly met Mill in her family's home from a young age and more recently through the women's suffrage movement, she addressed the letter to Taylor. As Mill's stepdaughter, Helen Taylor managed most of his correspondence, even writing some letters on his behalf herself.

Part of the correspondence between the two women is preserved at London School of Economics (LSE), which is located close to the Inns of Court and Chancery Lane and so not far from where some of the letters were written. The Women's Library at LSE has a comfortable and well-appointed reading room where an archivist brought me the file when I revisited in 2021. On my first visit, in 1990, it was a different room, simpler and plainer–though I really do not remember much from back then, except the excitement of reading the letters, scrambling to transcribe as many as possible, and all too quickly running out of time.

The first letter in the folder is dated 7 December 1872. Orme's 24th birthday was a few weeks away, her sojourn teaching in Wiltshire was a couple of years behind her, and her studies at University College were well established and already yielding prizes. Her letter begins formally, 'Dear Madam' and gets straight to the point.

> For some months I have been considering the best method of entering the legal profession. Professor and Mrs Cairnes, who have taken the kindest interest in the matter, approve my now writing to you for advice. Before stating my plans and difficulties it may be as well to explain, as shortly as possible, why I have undertaken what seems such a hopeless task. Since I have been actively working on the Women's Suffrage committee I have become convinced that we probably have many years work before us and that nothing assists the question so much as practical work done by women.

What an opening! Here was a clear statement of purpose, backed up by an impeccable academic reference. A gracious acknowledgment that the challenge was a hopeless one, and then a commitment—not to ideals, but to a political strategy and to hard practical work. Eliza went on to mention the name of Henry Fawcett, to repeat that of Professor Cairnes, and to add that of her brother-in-law, David Masson. She continued:

> I therefore resigned my office of secretary of the Exec. Comt^{ee} of the Lond. Nat. Soc. with the definite purpose of doing some practical work if possible and at the same time remaining a public supporter of the cause which seems to me to be of paramount importance. I have made up my mind to study law (1) because I see work to be done in explaining to women their real position from the legal point of view; (2) because it is a lucrative profession which ought to be open to women.

She was astute enough to realize that the quixotic decision to attempt a career in law might damage the reputation of the women's movement. ('The manner of making such an attempt as this has such an important effect that I should be quite willing to give up all public action if experienced friends thought the time ill-chosen or that I was an unsuitable person to commence it. Otherwise I am prepared to work steadily at the subject, quite independently of whether I am admitted as a student, and to gather support and sympathy as I go along'.) It was going to be a slow process and Eliza Orme, Helen Taylor, and John Stuart Mill all knew that for every instance of 'support and sympathy' there would be many more occasions for derision and undermining of the project.

She then apprised Taylor of her situation: 'In 1869 I passed the General Exam. at the Univ. of London and in 1870 took a Special Certificate in Physics and Chemistry. I intend taking similar certificates in Mathematics and Mechanics and in Political Economy next May, if possible. I am 24 years of age and am strong enough to work hard without its doing me any harm. I tell you these particulars because it seems unfair to ask your advice without giving you full information'. She was fudging her age, but only by a few weeks.

Having reminded Taylor of what she already knew, that Orme was a student at University College, the letter moved on to the nitty-gritty of legal training and credentials. These had nothing to do with academic education or the degree of Bachelor of Laws. To become a barrister, a young man had to spend three years as a pupil at one of the four Inns of Court. These were very old and tradition-bound institutions in central London, situated near the law courts. Their purpose was to reinforce and reproduce for succeeding generations the legal profession's culture of entitlement and privilege, which has been described by Ren Pepitone as 'a culture deeply resistant to women'. Calmly ignoring this incontrovertible fact, Orme noted for Taylor the pros and cons of applying to each of the Inns. Her own idea was to go to Gray's Inn, partly because 'there are so few benchers that it would be possible to bring pressure on each'. The letter closes with courtesies. In this initial communication, Orme is aiming for the more prestigious and powerful part of the legal profession, the bar. She might have tried to become a solicitor, where she would at least not have been putting on a wig and arguing in court in front of a learned judge. However that branch of the law was also restricted to men, this time by statute. Later on, she did consider that option, but at the beginning she coolly sifted the fitness of the several Inns of Court for her purposes.

Mill and Taylor replied a month later. The document that survives is a copy of their letter, with a note 'To Miss Orme, dictated by me'— that is dictated by Helen Taylor to John Stuart Mill. The Mill scholar Ann Robson says in an article that it is his handwriting. So Helen Taylor composed the letter, but she and Mill must have discussed the matter too. Taylor was positive, but she also mentioned two caveats in the first paragraph:

> There is no profession better suited for women to exercise, & none the study of which is better calculated for women's minds than that of the bar, & the only objection, therefore, that I see to it is the very great length of time that is likely to elapse before in the first place they can get admitted to it, & in the second place, before they will be able to practise.

If you look upon it as a pursuit, likely to enable a woman to attain to real superiority of mental power, & likely to enable her to be of use in advising women, as well as in shewing what women can do, I know of none which I should value more highly or perhaps even so highly. But I do not feel sure whether the effect on the public of the endeavor would be especially useful. I do not however think it would be injurious, & therefore the decision sh^d rest, I think, very much upon personal inclination.

Clearly Taylor thought that legal education was not a high priority for the women's movement. Not only would success take too long, but she foresaw—correctly—that 'the public' would not be supportive of 'the endeavor'. She continued:

As regards the question of which Inn of Court to apply to, it depends upon details of which neither Mr Mill nor myself feel ourselves competent to give any opinion without further consultation and advice. We expect to be in England early in next year, & if you do not make your decision before that time it would give us much pleasure to talk over the matter with you, & in the mean time we will consult those of our friends whose judgment we sh^d most rely on in such a matter.

I have long thought that it would be very useful if a firm of women solicitors could be established. But I am not sufficiently conversant with the details of the profession to know the relative difficulty of the obstacles to the success of a woman as a solicitor or as a barrister, happening the necessary capital for the beginning of a solicitor's business to be found. There is no doubt room for considerable development in England of the solicitor's portion of the law; and it would be very satisfactory if a woman were to lead the way in raising the solicitor's profession to a level with the barrister, as it sh^d be, instead of being regarded merely as a trade, as it is. How far these considerations might weigh in a choice between the two branches of the legal profession, I have not however considered from a practical point of view.

This was a diplomatic and somewhat hesitant response. (Not to mention remarkably unstrategic. Why ever should the admission of women to the legal profession serve to improve the status of solicitors vis à vis barristers?) Orme ignored their lack of enthusiasm in her follow-up letter of 28 April 1873. This offered details of an arrangement that had presumably been discussed, although not in the correspondence that survives. Those missing letters or conversations may also have contained Mill's commitment to pay Orme's fees at one of the Inns.

From Lincoln's Inn Fees to 'a Miniature Girton'

The initial arrangement, which in the end did not work out, was for Miss Orme to become a fee-paying pupil in the Lincoln's Inn chambers of John Savill Vaizey. That barrister knew John Westlake as a fellow-bencher and fellow-Liberal. Westlake's wife, the artist Alice Westlake, had met Orme through the women's movement and was willing to facilitate the introduction. Aspiring barristers were required to spend three years as pupils at one of the Inns, attached to a senior lawyer's chambers (office), eating a certain number of formal dinners and participating in other social rituals, as well as picking up some courtroom or litigation skills from the lawyers and clerks who lived and worked in these ancient and very masculine establishments. (They were not required to study for the academic LL.B. qualification.) For this extraordinary situation, the arrangement was fluid, perhaps six months or maybe a year, with only some of the rights and privileges of a pupil. Notably, it was imperative that Miss Orme become acquainted with her instructor's wife. Vaizey would have preferred to have two women pupils together, presumably for reasons of propriety, and there was some thought that Edith Simcox would participate. (Later, Mary Ellen Richardson joined the class.) While he did provide her with some professional guidance during their years together, Vaizey also required her assistance with his book on marriage settlements. It is not clear how extensive her participation in that project may have been, but Vaizey later acknowledged Orme's labour in preparing an 'elaborate index' of sixty-nine pages.

It is possible that Helen Taylor was less enthusiastic about supporting Eliza Orme than her stepfather would have been. John Stuart Mill died in the spring of 1873 and Taylor, while not withdrawing the offer of support, hinted that it would be difficult to find the money for Vaizey's fee. This put Orme in the awkward position of assuring her patron that she could cope easily with any delay. While she might really have needed the money, despite her family's wealth, I think it is more likely that Orme valued Taylor's sponsorship from more of a social and political perspective, given the latter's influence in both suffrage and Liberal circles. In any case, Taylor sent her £50 in October for the first six months, and Orme's training began. In a letter of December 1873, Orme reported that she would be 'unable to do anything profitable' until either the legislation or the professional norms changed: only simple wills and powers of attorney, not the more lucrative property conveyances. The legislation, she explained, explicitly forbade 'what is called "devilling" for other barristers'. Her judgment was that she 'must therefore work on with the hope of one day getting sufficient support to be admitted to an Inn'. Beneath Orme's humble approaches to Taylor and presumably to supporters like the Cairneses and Fawcetts (and perhaps to others where the correspondence is lost) she reveals the political motivation and strategy inherent in her ambition, aiming to 'get sufficient support' and even to 'bring pressure' on the benchers of one of the Inns.

Two years passed, and Orme was obliged to take on some pupils herself to make ends meet, and to avoid accepting any more money from Helen Taylor than was absolutely necessary (or perhaps politic). She helped Taylor with preparing a new edition of one of Mill's books, *Dissertations and Discussions*. By this time Mary Ellen Richardson, another London law student, had joined her in Vaizey's chambers, but the two women seem to have realized they were not getting very far. Someone introduced them to yet another barrister, William Phipson Beale, who told them they were wasting their time (and presumably their money). He advised Orme and Richardson to set themselves up independently, lease premises in Chancery Lane and offer their services to any barrister willing to pay for them, rather than tie themselves to one. This they did. Orme described Beale's plan in an August 1875 letter to Helen Taylor:

> He thinks we can become pupils of well-known men if we like at any time when the opportunity occurs and meantime we shall be gaining knowledge and friends by 'devilling' in our own chambers. It will be less expensive for us to take chambers than to read with a barrister and on the whole I am inclined to follow his advice. By taking rooms in Chancery Lane we shall excite less attention than if we were to try to engage any within one of the Inns of Court. Mr Beale is strongly of the opinion that we had better do some work before we make our claims to enter the profession and Miss Richardson and I both agree with him in this entirely.

To 'read' with a barrister as his 'pupil', the arrangement with Vaizey, would be a bit like undertaking an independent study project with a professor. But since male pupils were not so much reading (or studying) as apprenticing for a lifestyle that was limited to people of their gender, the arrangement was obviously not working very well for the two women. A barrister's 'devil', on the other hand, might be a pupil or a clerk; in the latter case their job was to prepare written legal work on behalf of the principal barrister. They might also go out and secure briefs from solicitors, and in those cases, they received a percentage of the principal barrister's fee. The clerk might work outside the rigid culture of the Inns of Court, not 'indoors' but 'outdoors', with chambers (an office) in Chancery Lane. Another loose category was that of 'legal assistant'. But there were no generally accepted terms, legal or informal, with which to describe a woman who was doing the work of a lawyer.

Three months later, Orme wrote again to Taylor, describing the set-up at 38 Chancery Lane as 'a miniature Girton', a phrase that evoked all the austere joys of the women's college at Cambridge. There were three of them, Eliza Orme, Mary Ellen Richardson, and a younger woman, Minnie Robertson. Minnie was a niece of Eliza Cairnes, preparing for examinations of her own. They had a little boy to run errands and 'a very respectable laundress' who looked after the establishment. (In the legal culture of the Inns of court, house servants were known as laundresses.) They all lived together too, in a house in Camden Road belonging to Richardson. As at Girton and other women's colleges, they could engage in tough disciplined intellectual work, argue politics and revel in literature—all the while drinking cocoa and toasting muffins at the fireplace—without having to perform the exacting and tedious social roles expected for leisured young women of their class.

Both Vaizey and Beale were offering work, as much as Orme and Richardson could handle, she told Helen Taylor. In Beale's case, he gave Orme half the fee he took for any draft that she could 'do completely enough to save him the trouble'. In his view, she told Taylor, if the women never signed the draft documents they prepared, 'but did them in the character of outdoor clerks' they could 'go on safely' even without being called to the bar. (Much later, in an 1893 article, Orme came to describe this kind of work in a more formal and above-board manner, in terms of working on the established legal principle of 'qui facit per alium, facit per se'—'He who acts through another does the act himself'. At this early stage, she was understandably more hesitant, and perhaps Beale was too.)

In December 1879 the *Women's Suffrage Journal* reported that 'a young lady has just sent in an application to the Incorporated Law Society'. This was the organization that controlled the accreditation of solicitors, quite separate from the Inns of Court that accredited barristers. However historians of the legal profession report that it was refused 'on grounds of sex'. I have never been able to determine whether this applicant was Eliza Orme, but it might have been. As it turned out, both the bar and the Law Society remained closed to women practitioners until after they were forced to open their doors in 1919.

More light on the work of conveyancing comes from Mary Jane Mossman, in her book on the first women lawyers in various jurisdictions. In England there was an elite category of lawyer known as the 'conveyancing barrister'. Their organization, the Institute of Conveyancing Barristers, was known as 'the forty thieves' and also operated as a dining club. These were high-powered men who handled complex and difficult property cases as well as estate law. Mossman speculates that:

> It seems likely that [Orme] was engaged by members of the Institute to provide legal opinions on land titles and to draft conveyancing documents, as a 'legal assistant'; such an arrangement would explain her receipt of 'half-fees'. Furthermore, Orme's acceptance as an assistant at the bar probably resulted from her ability to do highly competent and reliable legal work within this close-knit and highly specialised group of conveyancing barristers; indeed, her work for this group suggests that she was both accomplished and professional.

Even if William Phipson Beale did not himself dine among the 'forty thieves', he probably knew enough of them to put his protégée in touch with a lucrative source of work and income.

It seems pretty reasonable to speculate that this arrangement was humiliating, even though the 'practical' side of Eliza Orme's nature might have believed it was the best she and Mary Ellen Richardson could do and they should make the most of it. Much has changed in the century between their generation and mine, but there are resonances nevertheless: powerful male mentors who seemed affable but nevertheless could be capricious; barriers to promotion and other kinds of achievement; the pinpricks of discomfort and annoyance that accompany questions about one's competence When women lawyers in Britain began, in the lead-up to 2019, to look into their predecessors'

1919 achievement of equal status, many of the former focused on how judges smugly explained the latter's absence from courts by the lack of female toilet facilities in those establishments.

What did Orme and Richardson do all day? There is considerable evidence of a wide variety of professional activities going on in their chambers, beyond preparing conveyancing and estate-related documents for half-fees and doing less complex (and less legally restricted) work at full fee. In the latter category, Orme and Richardson were patent agents, and both were directors of a financial service business. The 1883 Patent Act had not only made the registration of intellectual property a more complex process than earlier; it had left the way open for qualified women by not limiting that process by formal qualifications. The Nineteenth Century Building Society was one of a class of important institutions concerned with mortgage lending. In addition to offering mortgages to individual house-purchasers, they also funded builders who were undertaking large-scale construction projects. The *Englishwoman's Review* reported in June 1880:

> The NCBS affords, we believe, the first instance of a Building Society, which numbers women among its directors ... The Society provides also special facilities to people of small means, by giving borrowers the right to make their repayments weekly instead of monthly, and it pays particular attention to the sanitary condition of property mortgaged to the Society. This last consideration is one which we think specially shows the advantage of having women among the responsible directors, as the sanitary condition of dwelling-houses particularly demands qualified female supervision.

All this sounds a long way from winning prizes for top marks in subjects as academic as political economy and Roman law. Many lawyers, then and now, make the transition from intellectually challenging course work at university to the mundane tasks of preparing documentation and so forth when they set up in practice. A smaller number make a more complex transition, from law school through practice and on to an apprenticeship in politics, either national or local. Perhaps the progressive policies of the Nineteenth Century Building Society might serve as evidence that Eliza Orme and Mary Richardson cherished aspirations in that direction? Or perhaps the *Englishwoman's Review* was being idealistic, and the women lawyers were in the mortgage business for the money.

A sidelight on Orme's financial arrangements, and the extent to which she would go to overcome obstacles, comes from her cousin Mabel Barltrop, who wrote with considerable indignation if not full understanding: 'She has become a barrister . . . and she has become so to prove that women are fully as capable as men to act in that capacity. But she is compelled by law only to take half fees, and is not even allowed the use of the Libraries for the use of those in the legal profession. She has to buy for herself all the expensive books, one set cost £40, the other day'. Half fees were an informal agreement, not a legal provision; and the books were presumably for the chambers as a whole, not just for herself. Still, it is worth noting that library access was apparently yet another of the masculine privileges reserved for members of the Inns of Court.

Discrimination and Challenges

In contrast to this modest attempt to wedge open the door of Chancery Lane by even a crack, other parts of Eliza Orme's life looked like one academic or journalistic success after another, but interspersed with one public challenge or mortification after another. In July 1872 she won first prize in Political Economy at University College. In December of that year, she ought to have received the Ricardo Scholarship in the same subject but it went to a London barrister, George Serrell. What is interesting here, and why we know about it, is the press reports. These indicated that the judges were Cairnes and Courtney, the winner was Mr Serrell, and that according to the judges Miss Eliza Orme had 'obtained a sufficient number of marks to qualify for the scholarship had she not had so powerful a competitor'. Perhaps the judges were quietly advocating for their protégée and expressing veiled disapproval of the injustice of the scholarship process. Having read those reports, the *Englishwoman's Review* dismissed Serrell as 'that old and accomplished prize-taker' and celebrated Miss Orme's proficiency. Three years later Orme reported to Helen Taylor that Hunter assured her he would have backed her for a 200-guinea scholarship in Roman Law, but it was offered by the Inns of Court and 'not open to women of course'. According to Hunter, the previous year's winning paper had been inferior to her own. Apparently undaunted (though these injustices must have stung), Eliza wrote two articles about 'University Degrees for Women' for *The Examiner*.

She knew how to defend herself when directly attacked. Late in 1876, University College London announced that Miss Orme had won the Hume Scholarship, a three-year award for the study of Jurisprudence. Soon after that, the college authorities received a letter from one Pascoe Daphne. This gentleman had missed the prize exam and felt entitled to request that he be allowed to write it anyway. Mr. Daphne further observed that Miss Orme ought not to have won the prize because he had not often seen her attending the lectures. When challenged, she pointed out to the authorities that she had sometimes arrived late, but had indeed been present despite having already sat the course of lectures (and applied for the same prize) the previous year. The scholarship designation remained unchanged. I will restrain my twenty-first century feminist indignation and just observe that there is evidence here of patience, not to say determination, in the face of severe and often humiliating obstacles.

Meanwhile the enterprise in Chancery Lane was a business success which began to draw notice, not all of it very desirable. An article by the *Sporting Gazette's* 'Man About Town' column of 24 June 1876 called attention to the two partners' distinction in the Roman Law examinations (Richardson came third and Orme first) but academic commendation soon gave way to matrimonial speculation: 'How long, I wonder, will the partnership last? Will they be proof against entering into that other foolish partnership in which the partners are of opposite sexes—known to mankind for some time past as matrimony? With such pretty faces and graceful figures, and with youth and health to boot, I am diffident of their long holding the fort of celibacy'. The same columnist wrote in November about the prospects for women doctors, lawyers, and clergy: 'Miss Orme and Miss Richardson, those eminent legal practitioners in Chancery-lane, are pretty enough to make any susceptible male rush into law merely for the pleasure of consulting them—and now here is Dr Mary Hogan ... When the physician and the lawyer come to us armed with all the wiles of woman, with beauty and youth to supplement their attacks, what hope is there for us? Will you turn parsons next?' No doubt there were equally unpleasant remarks being made among the barristers, solicitors, and clerks who populated Chancery Lane and the Inns of Court, including those who availed themselves of Orme's and Richardson's professional services.

'A Fine Chaos': Co-workers and Business Partners

Not much is known about Mary Ellen Richardson, except that she was elected a member of the London School Board from 1879 to 1885, and she lived with a woman, Jane Chessar. Richardson and Chessar were involved in the Somerville Club (as was Orme), and with a debating society and swimming clubs. Richardson does not seem to have completed the LL.B. degree, although she did well in some exam competitions as we have seen. In addition to sharing the chambers in Chancery Lane from the mid-1870s to the mid-1880s, she and Orme were both directors of the Nineteenth Century Building Society. Outside of the work environment, they were both part of the leadership of an Association to Promote Women's Knowledge of the Law, founded in 1878. This is something I would like to know more about (even though 'having knowledge of the law' was not the same thing as 'becoming a lawyer') but apart from a few press notices of meetings, little evidence seems to have survived. The *ODNB* essay on the education pioneer Jane Chessar says that Richardson was Honorary Treasurer of the organization. Chessar was also a member, as was Annie Besant. In any case, Richardson and Orme seem to have worked together for about a decade and lived together for at least part of that time. They both moved, with their families of origin, to the Bedford Park suburb of Chiswick in the eighties. A letter from Eliza Orme to the American suffrage pioneer Susan B. Anthony reveals that Richardson (and another woman, Miss Novelli) left the firm before February of 1884, to 'devote themselves ... to commercial speculations at Bedford Park'. The 'commercial speculation' was later advertised (including in Orme's own *Women's Gazette*) as The Stores, Bedford Park, a purveyor of toys, games, fancy boxes of chocolates, *patés de foies gras*, and turkeys from Ireland. I have not been able to track down any watertight documentation about Miss Novelli, but it is clear that not every woman who studied law continued to practice as a lawyer.

Thanks to that newsy letter to Susan B. Anthony, we also know that Reina Emily Lawrence had joined the firm by 1884. She too was a law student at University College. When Jessie Wright, an American lawyer, visited in 1888, the chambers (now located at 27 Southampton Buildings in Chancery Lane) still bore a brass plate marked 'Orme and

Richardson' but it was Reina Lawrence that she encountered ('a very pretty girl, with short, dark, curly hair, and she was scrawling away in the most business-like manner'). Wright describes the room as 'a fine chaos'—furnished with revolving chairs and a 'good sized office table' in the centre of the room, the table 'loaded with papers, pamphlets, books'; there was also a bookcase stocked with reports, and 'the floors were carpeted, a blazing soft coal fire burned in the open grate, two large windows were lowered from the top, a book case stocked with reports was behind me'. Prints of two paintings, one modern and one Renaissance, hung on the wall. Miss Orme was in the office next door, working with a client. An office boy ('black-eyed, in a gray suit, stiff as a ramrod') stood next to Lawrence at the table, waiting for orders. Wright sketched this word-portrait of the firm for her fellow American members of the Equity Club, adding that 'Miss Orme is fine; a first-rate kind of woman, and nobody could have been more kind and cordial than she has been to me'.

Fig. 4 Reina Emily Lawrence (n.d., photographer unknown), ©John Partington, London. Reproduced with permission. http://www.pjohnp.me.uk/famhist/ lawrence-re.pdf

A fictional description of a London professional women's office, intriguingly similar to Wright's of 27 Southampton Buildings, can only be a tentative attribution. It comes from Bernard Shaw in the text of his 1893 play *Mrs Warren's Profession*. The profession in question was that of prostitute and brothel-manager, but in the play it is set in contrast to the professional life and values of Mrs Warren's adult daughter. Vivie Warren is Cambridge-educated (in mathematics) and works with a partner in Chancery Lane chambers. The partner, Honoria Fraser is somewhat older than Vivie, in the business of actuarial calculations and conveyancing, resolutely single and financially independent. Setting the scene for the chambers of 'Fraser and Warren', Shaw noted: 'There is a double writing table in the middle of the room, with a cigar box, ash pans, and a portable electric reading lamp almost snowed up in heaps of papers and books. This table has knee holes and chairs right and left and is very untidy'. The Shaw scholar Michael Holroyd thinks Vivie might have been modelled on Eliza Orme, presumably on the strength of Shaw's remark on one occasion that the 'original' of Vivie 'heads a party which denounces my plays as disgusting'. (Close enough, although Orme was not technically head of the Women's Liberal Federation, which was not technically a party.) On another occasion, Shaw mentioned a different woman, Beatrice Potter, as his model. The play was not performed in England for many years, because of its 'immoral' (or as Shaw puts it, 'unpleasant') aspects, so it is unlikely that Orme was aware she might have been used as a model for Honoria Fraser. But now that so much more is known about Eliza Orme, I would suggest that it might be of interest to Shaw scholars to explore the connection once again. In any case, 27 Southampton Buildings sounds like an attractive place to work.

There is a rather strange footnote to the story of Eliza's relationship with Helen Taylor. A whole year after Orme's last surviving letter (which described her 'miniature Girton', sought Taylor's support for a protégée's education and bragged a little about some of her own academic accomplishments), Taylor received a letter from Mary Ellen Richardson. It contained a cheque for £100, repaying funds that had been sent to Orme in three increments. Richardson insisted that Orme had spoken of Taylor and Mill with deep gratitude, 'but after the events of the past 2 months' (this was December 1876) 'I do not choose that she should longer remain indebted to you, for what, I can with no inconvenience send to you for her'. Taylor replied, outraged and (at least in the draft version which is all that survives) rather incoherent. She declined to receive the money and denied that she knew who Richardson was. Ann Robson speculates that this had something to do with Helen Taylor's anti-clerical views, which had been publicized during her recent election to the London School Board. Given what I know of Eliza Orme, that seems unlikely, and research by Jane Martin (on Chessar) reveals that Taylor and Richardson, both school board members, clashed on several occasions. It is also possible that Orme and Richardson had, by this time, come to realize that Helen Taylor's support for their larger ambitions was lukewarm at best, and perhaps even a liability. The little incident is curious, a reminder of how much about these women remains unknown.

Although I cannot measure the relative proportions of each aspect, it seems that Eliza's working life in her thirties—roughly the 1880s—fell into three parts. She worked in the Chancery Lane office alongside Mary Richardson and later Reina Lawrence, preparing conveyancing documents for barristers as well as organizing financing for homeowners through the Nineteenth Century Building Society and helping inventors to secure patents. At the same time, she lectured extensively, wrote articles for the periodical press, and engaged in several organizations aimed at improving public life in various ways: not just women's suffrage and women's employment, but world peace, proportional representation, Home Rule for Ireland, and other causes. Some of these activities would have been paid, while others were, no doubt, done gratis. And thirdly, there were her studies. Most years, Orme's name appears on the register of University College, and in 1880 she passed the initial LL.B. exam. This was the first of two; the second came in 1888. Once her academic studies were finished, however, and the degree obtained, Orme seems to have committed more of her energies to party politics. Her friend Sophia Fry had founded the Women's Liberal Federation (WLF) in 1886, and Orme immediately took on a leadership position. From 1888 to 1892, she was the editor of the WLF's newspaper, the *Women's Gazette and Weekly News* (*WGWN*). I will return to several of these activities in Chapters 5 and 6, and just note for now that she always did more than serve as a barristers' devil.

This chapter is entitled 'the commitment to law' but it ends with a question. Just how committed to law was Eliza Orme? Or perhaps a better way to phrase it would be to ask what the practice of law meant to her. To the extent that law is an academic discipline and an intellectual exercise, I believe she enjoyed it and was good at it. (Her massive and painstaking index to Vaizey's book on the law of marriage settlements might be evidence of that arcane pleasure.) But law is also a career and an identity, and it can be a vocation. She told Helen Taylor she wanted to enter the profession partly to help women clients with gender-specific legal challenges, and partly because it was lucrative and should be open to women practitioners. Given the gender limitations on being a barrister or solicitor in her time, both ambitions were really impossible. (Slightly mystified press reports at the time of her 1888 degree, especially those reporting on her quasi-professional labours along with the academic kudos, are evidence of this ambiguity.) But law can also be a stepping-stone to political power, with the call to the bar serving as one step in a life plan that includes journalism, networking, the paying of social dues, the testing of a reputation for party loyalty, then eventually nomination, campaigning, election, and a seat in the House of Commons, perhaps even one in the Prime Minister's cabinet. I have not found evidence that this was Eliza Orme's ambition. It is only my speculation. But in the 1870s and 1880s, neither she nor anyone else knew how painfully long it was going to take before women in Britain could reasonably articulate this kind of objective. She told Jessie Wright in 1888 that 'when four or five women were ready to apply for admission to the bar, they would do so'. Wright added: 'She says she thinks things look more hopeful now than ever, and that several of the benchers are already in favor of [women] being admitted – not as solicitors ... but as barristers'. For an optimist with a high opinion of her own capabilities, perhaps Eliza Orme's larger aspirations seemed, that year as she turned forty, eminently reasonable and still on track. But it remains impossible to know whether the law was her ambition in life, or merely a stepping-stone to another goal, because we know so little of her private hopes and dreams, of her personal likes and dislikes, her prejudices and partialities.

4. Private Life

Eliza Orme thought Christmas cards were stupid. She much preferred 'a nice hearty greeting' in the form of a letter, 'instead of one of those senseless cards that we are inundated with—Cats—heartseases—frogs in tail coats—castles—all manner of things in earth and heaven with the ever recurring "happy Xmas" printed beneath'. So, with an almost audible snort, she told her friend Sam Alexander in 1887, in response to his having written a proper letter to her mother. She also delighted in funny or poignant happenings, especially if they involved the Irish dialect: In an 1889 letter to Sam from Ireland, she observed of 'these fascinating Celts' that 'they use our longest words in the most eccentric way—just off the exact grammatical line—and it results in a mixture of pathos and humour which conquers me "entirely"'. She continued: 'Yesterday I was talking to a poor tenant who lives in a poor mud hovel not fit for a pig. Wife and innumerable children. I had been thinking that if I had been in his place or in his wife's place suicide would have been my cure at once. But when we left the cabin he attached himself in a most sociable way and discoursed politics with such intelligence that I began to see why his life was interesting enough to keep him alive'. She took even more pleasure in beloved friends. Later in life, she recalled seeing in the new year of 1900 with Sam and his dog, and some of her family including their own dog Rhoda: 'we walked down Tulse Hill and fancied we heard St Pauls Cathedral ringing in the new century. We heard all sorts of strange noises and the vague hum of the great city'. Eliza's letters to Sam have little to do with her status as a professional person making her mark in public life. They do, however, give us a whisper of the voice that her friends and family knew, a tart but warm, laughing but thoughtful voice that she must consciously have set aside when dealing with barristers, speaking on suffrage platforms, and strategizing at Liberal committee meetings.

     https://doi.org/10.11647/OBP.0392.04

To put a face to that voice, we can look at the photograph taken in 1889, when Eliza Orme was forty, at The Cameron Studio, in Mortimer Street in central London. (That was not the studio of the famous Victorian photographer Julia Margaret Cameron, but of her son, Henry Herschel Hay Cameron, who specialized in portraiture.) She turns to one side, faintly smiling and serene, her dark hair pulled up and back from a high forehead. She has a strong nose and chin, elegant eyebrows. She is conventionally dressed, as befits her decided views on the extremes of attire adopted by some of her contemporaries who styled themselves the 'new women'. I wonder how it came to be taken. Did Cameron invite her, or did Eliza commission the portrait herself, perhaps to commemorate achieving the law degree a few months earlier? I think it must have been a private commission because I have never seen a nineteenth-century reproduction of this photograph—although now (thanks to me) it adorns various websites celebrating the first women lawyers in Britain and it was even reproduced in colour, in oil paint on canvas (by the artist Toby Ursell), as part of one such celebration. A framed print hangs in my office. I am forever grateful to Pierre and Hélène Coustillas, for giving me a scan of the original. They told me it had been inscribed by Eliza to her Australian nephew David Orme Masson and inherited by Professor Masson's granddaughter Jenny Young. So it seems likely that Aunt Eliza had a few copies made for family members and friends. The Massons in Edinburgh might have received a copy, as well as the Bastians in Manchester Square, and the Foxes in Cornwall. Maybe one sat on a table in Reina Lawrence's Belsize Avenue home. Perhaps another adorned the Oxford rooms of the scholar Samuel Alexander. Eliza may have had a whole 'other family' in the town of Buxton: perhaps they, whoever they were, received a copy of the portrait too. But this is all speculation: she remains elusive. Her public persona—which we will come to in Chapter 5—was, necessarily, so severe (although the severity was tempered by an acerbic humour that I think she cultivated) that the giddiness, the wit, and the warmth of her few surviving personal letters come as a delightful surprise. I like to think the photograph shows a bit of both.

Fig. 5 Eliza Orme (1889, The Cameron Studio), ©The estate of Jenny Loxton Young.

When I wrote my 1989 article, I said that 'no diary, letters, or other personal papers of Eliza Orme have survived'. Even back then, I should have known better. Most certainly I should have known about the businesslike letters to Helen Taylor at the London School of Economics, but I was distracted by other commitments and interests and had come to believe there was nothing to be found, so I stopped looking very hard. In my defence, I was never part of the network of historians working on the mid-Victorian women's movement, where I might have got wind of the Taylor collection from a colleague. It would not be reasonable, though, to blame myself for not finding her letters to Samuel Alexander, even though at the time they were safely ensconced with that philosopher's papers at the John Rylands Library in Manchester. Those I came across quite serendipitously, at home in 2020, through combining her name in a search engine with that of another of Alexander's correspondents. The Rylands archivists had recently put a finding aid to his papers online, and the algorithm did the rest. (The archivists noted that she was one of the few correspondents to address him as 'Sam') Both the Taylor and the Alexander letters have to be seen on site at the relevant library, or else by way of a digital scan supplied by the staff in charge.

Whereas her letter of 1884 to Susan B. Anthony (the one that gives news of Eliza's mother as well as of her colleagues) was published in the National Woman Suffrage Association's *Report* of their Washington convention, has been digitized, and is online. A few others have turned up in similarly unexpected places, but there is still not much. She wrote dozens of letters to George Gissing, but he kept none of them. I would give a lot to see any intimate letters (or even business letters) she might have written to Reina Lawrence. But if they ever existed those letters were most likely either tossed in a waste-paper basket or kept only to be destroyed later, in the course of a wartime paper drive.

The other thing that was unavailable when I began this research in the 1980s was the internet. Three decades and more after my first encounter with Eliza Orme, and my initial pursuit of her in the pages of Gissing's published diary and letters, much is now available to me in my home office. I am glad I made those delightful but laborious visits—to London archives and record offices, to Somerset House where wills were lodged, to Warwick University in Coventry to see Clara Collet's papers, and to the Public Record Office in Chancery Lane to see the census records—but even gladder that there is now an alternative. Census and other government records like birth and death certificates and wills are now readily available, for a small fee. The British Newspaper Archive and periodicals databases make millions of contemporary words, some of them identifying her by name, available through academic libraries. I have also become adept at online searches, entering either her full name, or 'Miss Orme', or sometimes just her surname, in juxtaposition with another word or phrase that identifies a person or institution. Much of what appears that way is about her public life, of course, but when she encountered someone who later became well-known—Christina Rossetti, Susan B. Anthony, John Stuart Mill, Beatrice Webb, to name a few—then the encounter might have been captured in some nineteenth-century book, and hence in the Internet Archive. Remarkable. But, accessible as all these things are, you first have to frame the question, and propose the juxtaposition.

The borderline between public and private is blurred when a woman's accomplishment is unthinkable and most of the evidence undiscoverable. In that sense, the paid legal work in Chancery Lane in these decades might almost be considered part of her private life: those discreet services to barristers, taking on their intricate jobs at half-fees, were not advertised or (as far as I know) documented. Her availability must have been made known by word of mouth. For a couple of decades of her long life she was also a minor public figure, especially from the mid-1880s to the mid-90s beginning with the foundation of the Women's Liberal Federation and then her appointment to a Royal Commission on Labour and later to a government committee on prisons. However she was not well enough known to develop an indelible reputation, like Josephine Butler or Millicent Fawcett. Indeed, the people who memorialized those other leaders may have consciously erased Orme's name from the feminist record, or maybe subconsciously forgotten to include it, for reasons we will see in Chapter 7 with the messy split in the WLF that happened in 1892. At that time, the name of 'Miss Orme' was in the public eye while 'Eliza' was careful to keep her private life just that—private.

Family and Childhood

Census records show that Charles Orme was twenty-six when he married Eliza Andrews in 1832; she was sixteen. Directories and press advertisements reveal that he was a businessman in the liquor trade, a distiller with premises in Blackfriars that he had inherited from his own father. The business obviously prospered, since Charles supported a large family of eight children, a wife, a sister-in-law, and four live-in servants. Eliza gave birth to her first child at seventeen and her last at forty-one. As 'Mrs Charles Orme', she became well known for the informal salon she hosted in their house on Avenue Road in Regent's Park on Friday evenings. Her guests included some of the leading artists and intellectuals of mid-Victorian London as well as people in the women's suffrage movement. A third adult later joined the household in the shape of Georgina Patmore, the senior Eliza Orme's ten-years-younger sister and a widow. I cannot help but notice some intriguing parallels between the Ormes' arrangements and the central characters of A. S. Byatt's wonderful novel tracing a handful of complex families from the 1890s through to the 1920s, *The Children's Book*.

At this point, I must pause to say 'mea culpa' on my own behalf, but perhaps also gently critique the careless scholarship of some long-dead aficionados of the mid-Victorian literary world. In more than one sketch of Eliza Orme, I have followed those gentlemen in noting that the lawyer's mother was governess to Elizabeth Barrett Browning before her marriage. This was fun: it was name-dropping, it was colourful—but it was not true and I should have checked up sooner. I based the error on historical accounts of Barrett Browning's connections with the Pre-Raphaelite Brotherhood. As it turns out, the poet kept in touch with a former governess by the name of Charlotte Orme (always referred to as 'Mrs Orme' by Victorian convention), and it was that lady who effected an all-important introduction to the brotherhood. To confuse matters and explain how the mistake was made in the first place, Eliza Orme senior did have a rich network of relationships with the Pre-Raphaelites herself. A University College London Ph.D. thesis by Scott Lewis was my source for the correct information.

Back to the firmer ground of census records.

Eliza and her sister Beatrice were the youngest of the Orme children, so much so that their niece Flora Masson was a year older than Beatrice, and their nephew David just a few months younger when they were all still living together in that capacious house. The eldest son, Charles Edward Orme (1833–1912) became a surgeon; he remained a bachelor and lived with his parents for many years, and latterly with Eliza and Beatrice. The second son (and fifth child) was Campbell Orme, also a surgeon, again a bachelor. Born in 1842, six years before Eliza, he studied at St Bartholomew's Hospital; in 1871 he was serving as 'medical assistant' at a mental hospital. Campbell Orme died at forty-one, on board a Royal Mail ship at Rio de Janeiro. At that point he was a medical officer with the Guinea Coast Gold Mining Company. Orme told Susan B. Anthony that the death had been a 'great shock' to her mother, adding 'My brother was not publicly known at all, but he was deeply valued in his own family and after a long illness we thought he had recovered'.

Eliza Orme senior had already lost a child when Campbell died in 1883. Helen Foster Orme died in 1857 at the age of twenty when Eliza was only eight. Helen was a childhood friend of the poet Christina Rossetti. The record shows that she died in Hemel Hampstead, Hertfordshire, an agricultural market town outside London. Their sister Rosaline Masson named a child after Helen. Apart from these fragments, I know nothing of Helen's life. I wonder if Eliza Orme's poem, 'Song', might have been written to evoke her memory; it was first published in *The Examiner* in 1875: 'I'm thinking of a fair face, The fairest ever seen; And I sigh good-bye to summer, And the glory of the green'. It could be about anybody, but it might be about Helen.

The Ormes' eldest daughter was Rosaline, born three years after their marriage. In 1854, when Rosaline was nineteen and marrying David Masson, Christina Rossetti described the bride to a friend as 'pretty, clever I imagine, and indescribably winning'. Rosaline and David lived with the family in the Avenue Road house for many years, and she gave birth to two children there before her husband was appointed to an important post in Edinburgh. The next daughter was Helen, then Julia Augusta Orme (1840–1928), who married the physician and psychologist-neurologist Henry Charlton Bastian (he later became Professor of Pathological Anatomy and of Clinical Medicine in University College London). The Bastians, in their turn, lived at Avenue Road after their 1866 marriage (and after the Massons had moved out); they were still there with two children for the 1871 census when Eliza was away teaching in Wiltshire. When they got their own London home it was in Manchester Square. The Bastians had five children. The third married sister was Olivia Blanche (1844–1930); she was just four years older than Eliza. Blanche married Howard Fox, a merchant and ship agent, and lived in Falmouth, in Cornwall. Howard came from a Quaker family; he was American consul in Falmouth and also acted as consul for Ecuador, Sweden, Norway and Denmark. There is evidence in Eliza's and Beatrice's later lives of a close relationship with the Cornwall family.

Last of all came Beatrice, born the same year that Helen died, 1857. Her oldest sibling Charles was twenty-five, her sister Eliza was eight. This daughter's full name was Beatrice Masson Orme, just as some of the Masson, Bastian, and Fox children were given 'Orme' as their middle names. Beatrice attended University College London from 1879 to 1881 but does not seem to have graduated. She was active in various women's rights causes, notably the Women's Liberal Federation alongside her sister. Beatrice and Charles Edward Orme both lived with Eliza for decades, in Eliza's homes in Chiswick (Bedford Park) and later Brixton (Tulse Hill). There is evidence in the letters to Sam Alexander and in George Gissing's diary that the two sisters were close. It might be tempting to think that Beatrice's role in her sister's life became some combination of the ones that Eliza described in an 1897 article about how a professional woman organizes her life: 'She has a house of her own with servants, one of whom is very probably a lady help or companion housekeeper, whose domestic tastes make the position pleasant as well as profitable. And very likely she helps a younger sister or niece to enter upon a life as useful and honourable as her own'.

It is difficult to discover much about schooling for the girls in this family and might be tempting to think that with such intellectual parents, aunts and uncles, brothers-in-law, and visitors, they hardly needed it. What we do know is that three of the sisters attended Bedford College for Women, as I mentioned in Chapter 2. We are on firmer ground with university education since both Eliza and Beatrice attended University College. As for their brothers, Charles Edward's medical education as a surgeon would not have involved university training. It is unclear what qualifications Campbell Orme had to be a 'medical officer' but I have found no record of a degree. Certainly Eliza's LL.B. was the highest educational attainment achieved by anyone in the family.

The Orme family had numerous cousins on the Andrews side. One who left a record of her visits to Avenue Road was Mabel Barltrop, who came to stay in the 1880s when Eliza was busy with her practice of law, her academic studies, and her political interests. Mabel was quite friendly with both Charles Edward and Beatrice Orme; she referred to the latter as 'Bix'. Perhaps this was a family nickname, and if so it is delightful, if disconcerting, to learn that *en famille* Eliza was 'Sili'. Despite using the goofy nickname, Mabel was in considerable awe of Eliza, who introduced her to people and took her along to lectures and suffrage meetings, even a private preview of an art exhibition at the Royal Academy. Mabel wrote to her fiancé that Eliza was someone who 'should be worshiped' and 'a darling', adding 'You cannot fail to like and admire her. I think hers a lovely character, always doing something for somebody'. Mabel's indignation about Eliza's exclusion from law libraries at the Inns of Court also appears in this letter. (For the sources of these quotes and the extraordinary life of Mabel Barltrop, see *Octavia Daughter of God: The Story of a Female Messiah and her Followers*, by Jane Shaw. But that really is another story.)

Apart from the dubious documentation of the names of Charles Orme's sisters Caroline (her husband was Henry Richard Brett, her dates were 1804–1867, and she had two children) and Emily (born about 1821) on genealogy websites, I have not found evidence of aunts, uncles, or cousins on the Orme side of the family.

The Ormes lived in three houses over the half-century I am interested in. All eight of the children were born at 16 Regent Villas (later 81 Avenue Road) in the Regent's Park area of north London. For those who orient themselves to London through women's suffrage landmarks, the house was not far from Langham Place. Others might find it more compelling to know that property on that street is now among the highest-priced in the United Kingdom. At some point in the early 1880s, they moved to a new suburb in the west-London area of Chiswick, called Bedford Park (number 2, The Orchard, to be exact). By that time the family had dwindled to the two parents and their three unmarried offspring Charles Edward, Eliza, and Beatrice, plus a couple of servants. Bedford Park was a railway suburb, which made it convenient for Eliza to commute to Chancery Lane and to her many political meetings around the country. Mary Ellen Richardson lived in the neighbourhood too, operating her retail business nearby. Bedford Park was also a newly developed garden suburb, which quickly became popular with writers who thought of themselves as 'aesthetes', and with a new generation of the same sort of artists and intellectuals who had frequented the house in Avenue Road. Then in the mid-1890s, after both parents had died, the three siblings moved to yet another new suburb, into the house at 118 Upper Tulse Hill, in the south London district of Lambeth.

I made a pilgrimage to Avenue Road early in my researches on Eliza Orme, and later went to Bedford Park in Chiswick. When I visited Tulse Hill it was in the 1990s, a rather turbulent time in the history of London's race relations. I remember choosing Sunday morning for the expedition, feeling anxious about my safety, and taking great satisfaction in finding the house, a little shabby at that point but a substantial two-storey establishment. Although I am not now certain that it was the same one, since house numbering has changed.

Eliza Orme's letters to Samuel Alexander indicate that she regarded both his family and Reina Lawrence's as part of her own circle of aunts and cousins, siblings and nieces and nephews, and felt at home in their homes. Mysteriously, one of those letters to Sam hints at yet another such family. In the busy year of 1888, she told her friend that she had been taking care of her father 'while Mamma and Beatrice are at Brighton.

They return tomorrow and I join my other family at Buxton. I wish there were a few less of the Sol Cohen tribe there but Aunt Loo makes up for a few of them'. Then she was heading for Edinburgh for a family wedding and looking forward to 'another luxurious rest at Buxton' before making a political trip to Ireland. Buxton is a spa town in Derbyshire, in the Peak District of England. Who the Cohens were, what was objectionable about Sol Cohen or his connection, and what the charms of Aunt Loo might have been, I have no idea. And it is not for a lack of trolling through census records and old newspapers to try to figure it out. My searches did reveal one possibility: Reina Lawrence's father was the nephew of a New York businessman by the name of Lewis Cohen. But both Lawrence and Cohen are common names. Perhaps the people in Buxton were what we now call a 'chosen family'.

Friends and (perhaps) Lovers

If Eliza Orme was in a long-term intimate relationship with anyone, the most likely candidate is Reina Emily Lawrence. The sources that were first available to me did not provide any clues, and I must admit that back then I was probably thinking more in terms of men in her life. I had missed the 2008 biography of Gissing by Paul Delany, who stated definitely (but with no footnote) that the two women were a couple: 'She never married, apart from a "Boston marriage" with Harry Lawrence's sister', he wrote. The term refers to a long-term intimate relationship between independent women who might, or might not, think of themselves as lesbians. In 2014 when I encountered Mary Jane Mossman, she told me about a new biography of George Gissing that referred to the relationship. I now realize that she meant Delany's, since she mentioned it in a footnote to a 2016 article. But at the time, I assumed she was talking about the three-volume *Heroic Life of George Gissing* by Pierre Coustillas, published in 2011–12. I looked that one up and discovered Coustillas had referred to Lawrence as Orme's 'intimate friend'. Knowing that the phrase can denote anything from a close friendship to a fully-fledged sexual relationship, I decided to ask Professor Coustillas, with whom I was by this time corresponding. He replied that in all the years that he and Hélène Coustillas had been researching Orme as an associate of Gissing's, they 'had never for one moment entertained the idea of a sexual relationship' between her and Reina Lawrence. I have since corresponded with Paul Delany, who was unable to supply any further information about his offhand remark. So there is still no hard evidence, one way or another.

Unlike Coustillas, I am quite prepared to entertain the idea. Beyond whatever offhand tittle-tattle Delany picked up in his researches on Gissing's associates, there is the circumstantial evidence that when Eliza drafted her will in 1885, she made Reina her executor. At that time, Eliza was thirty-eight, in practice with Mary Ellen Richardson. Reina was twenty-four, still a law student herself. In a very short time, Miss Lawrence joined Miss Orme in the Chancery Lane law chambers. Jessie Wright's visit in 1888 is evidence for that. When Eliza died in 1933, Reina duly executed her will, which had designated her as heir to Eliza's real estate and residuary personal estate (the money and securities were left to Beatrice). In itself, the half-century duration of that friendship offers its own kind of evidence of intimacy, perhaps sexual, perhaps not. On the other hand, the two women never seem to have lived together under the same roof, except perhaps on holiday.

Reina Emily Lawrence (1861–1940) was born in New York City, third of the nine children of John Moss Lawrence, a London-born merchant who made his fortune in the business of printing playing-cards. The family was Jewish. It would be intriguing to know more about the mother, Emily Lawrence, who was born in Jamaica into the Asher family, and was married to someone called Mills before she married John Lawrence. Two of Reina's siblings are notable: Esther Lawrence ('Essie') who became head of Froebel College, the progressive teacher-training establishment, and Henry Walton ('Harry') Lawrence, who became a partner with the publisher A. H. Bullen. (Lawrence and Bullen published some of George Gissing's books, and it was while smoking at their after-dinner table that the novelist first encountered Eliza Orme, though he perhaps did not know that she was a family friend.) The Lawrences lived at 37 Belsize Avenue, in Hampstead, not far from the Ormes' Avenue Road home. Eliza's letters to Sam Alexander refer chummily to 'the Belsize flock', or to 'spending every spare minute at Belsize lately', especially around the time when the father died in 1888. Much later, in 1916 when Beatrice was sixty-seven (and there was a war on), she and Beatrice went to Belsize and 'led a lazy and luxurious life there for ten weeks'.

Reina Lawrence earned her own LL.B. degree in 1893. Apart from working in the Chancery Lane chambers both before and after that event, she was active in local politics, serving on the Hampstead Distress Committee whose mandate was to help unemployed people. In 1907, when Lawrence was in her mid-forties, Parliament passed a Qualification of Women Act which enabled women to be elected to Borough and County Councils. In a by-election that same year Lawrence became the first woman elected as a councillor in London. She told voters that she was particularly interested in issues of housing, swimming baths, and infant mortality and assured them that she was not a suffragette. She was a candidate again but not re-elected in 1909, and continued to work, along with her sisters and others, on what Eliza described in a 1916 letter to Sam as 'care committees' and 'similar philanthropic efforts', adding 'Reina has knowledge and experience and a capacity for seeing two sides of a question which is invaluable in this sort of work'.

I would like to end this section with an authoritative account of Reina's 'intimate friendship'—whatever its terms—with Eliza, but that is not possible. For the record, I do think it was probably a lesbian partnership, but I do not know, and incontrovertible evidence is difficult to come by. It is easier to show that they were political allies. In a letter to Sam (undated but possibly 1887, or maybe late in 1889), Eliza reported on a visit to Lyndhurst, in the New Forest area of Hampshire. Both Reina and Essie Lawrence were part of the party, with other members of that family including a baby grandchild. They all went to Ringwood by train, had lunch in 'a pretty Inn on the fringe of the woods' and then walked about twelve miles: 'by keeping our shadows before us struck right through furze and thicket to Lyndhurst to a cosy tea in the Crown'. On another day they all went to a 'radical demonstration', that is, a political meeting where one of the speakers was the Irish Fenian John O'Connor Power. Eliza adds: 'Reina and I do all sorts of Home Rule Union work rather like needle-work on Saturday. That is we do not exhibit unnecessarily before the eyes of the Boss'. It is not clear whether 'the Boss' was Reina's formidable but clearly beloved mother, or one of her siblings, or someone else. Strategizing about the politics of Ireland is hardly intimate talk, but there is something about the suggestion of Saturdays and needle-work (that most female and feminine of occupations) that sounds like it excludes others from the conversation.

That's about it for suggestive language in the Alexander letters, with one remarkable exception. If Reina was present at an 1890 house party in the Scottish highlands, then we might infer that the coded language Eliza used on that occasion, about women wishing to spend their time untrammelled by male relatives, was a roundabout way of saying they wanted to be alone with people who understood and accepted the nature of their relationship. The letter of 27 August 1890, from Ballachulish in the highlands of Scotland, is the most intriguing (and frustrating) of all Eliza's letters to Sam. I have expended hours of energy, trying to track down the people she alludes to, to little or no avail. The tone of the letter, like many of the others, is light-hearted and teasing. The whole thing may well be an elaborate in-joke. Here it is, with irrelevant parts elided:

My dear Mr Alexander [she normally addressed him as 'Dear Sam' so this is mock formality]. Your Aunt has asked me to reply to your letter received today as she thinks that one who is an old friend will perhaps be able to do so more easily than she could and she does not think you would care for any of your cousins to be mixed up in the matter. She wishes you to understand in the first place that she values highly the warm family affection which prompts your earnest desire to come to Ballachulish ... But it is best to speak quite plainly and so I have to tell you, she cannot do with you here at all. I am sure if you think of it you will see for yourself how totally unsuitable it would be. We are a party of ladies and just one man would be a mere clergyman`s tea-party. It is not that your Aunt does not respect men, and even boys, in their proper place but there is no denying that they are a terrible nuisance when women want to enjoy a real change and holiday. We spend our time quite informally taking our meals how and when we please. We dress in tam-o-shanters and ulsters without any worry or conventionality. We take long walks and roving expeditions almost every day. To be obliged to consider the whims and necessities of a man, however much we may like him personally, would be to change our present ease into the stiffness of Scarboro' or Brighton. Do not suppose from what I have said that we are at all intellectually idle. We heard by chance of Cardinal Newman's death and have frequently repeated 'Lead Kindly Light' to one another since. A copy of the Woman's Gazette dated August 2nd has been lying on the table quite prominently and an odd volume of Waverley belongs to the house and can be read by us if we feel inclined to study Scotch history.

This is an extraordinary letter for a woman to write to a man in the 1890s, and very difficult to interpret. In the first place, I cannot work out which aunt she is referring to. Not the one who came to live with Sam and his mother from Australia, because that did not happen until later. Possibly the one who lived in Wiltshire, who wrote him a couple of letters in the 1890s, according to the handlist with the Alexander papers at the John Rylands Library. I cannot help wondering if this is an honorary aunt, and in particular if it might be Emily Lawrence, Reina's mother, to whom Eliza refers affectionately in other letters as 'the Old Lady' (or just, the OL). But really the aunt does not matter. What matters is a 'party of ladies' who insist that they must be free to dress as they please (ulsters are a kind of informal overcoat with a cape, and tam o'shanters are flat hats originating in Scotland), eat meals when they feel like it, and go for long walks on a whim. All in the freedom of a rural cottage in the highlands, far from 'the stiffness of Scarborough or Brighton' (both seaside resort towns frequented by the two families). As for the remarks about Cardinal Newman's poem and Walter Scott's novel, I believe they are meant to be sarcastic, as is the reference to the *Women's Gazette and Weekly News* of which Eliza was editor at this point.

Of course it is tempting to suppose that the 'party of ladies' indulged in some sexual intimacy that had to be concealed from the masculine gaze. On the other hand, it is a bit mind-boggling to think of such goings-on at a family outing which included members of at least two generations— though certainly not impossible. More likely, though, this is the same kind of arch humour that Eliza deployed in her other letters (such as the one quoted in the Prologue, where she implored him to attend a party at the Belsize Avenue Lawrence home and drink Oscary Wildey lemonade) but meant in this case to gently let Sam know why he would be unwelcome, while at the same time reminding him of everyone's strong affection. If I am right, her forthrightness is noteworthy here. How many women of her generation were in a position to tell a man not to show up, merely because she and her friends would prefer a few days free of deferring to the sensibilities of people of his gender? None of the other members of the house party are named, so it is impossible to be sure, but I like to think they were the Lawrence women, mother and daughters, on a jaunt with their family friend Eliza Orme.

Samuel Alexander was Jewish, as were the Lawrences. He may have met them when he came to England from Australia, or perhaps he knew

There is evidence for the genuine friendships that existed among Eliza Orme, Sam Alexander, and Reina Lawrence, an intimacy that extended to members of all three friends' families. That evidence takes the form of Eliza's letters to Sam and her choice of Reina as executor, along with a few fragments from other sources. But it is certain that Eliza Orme had other close friends apart from the Lawrence and Alexander families. If letters from Mary Richardson had survived, or from someone in the 'other family' at Buxton, they would have shown just as warm and supportive a relationship as those with Sam Alexander. One close connection that she mentions in a letter to Sam is with the Liberal journalist and politician Auberon Herbert: 'The most unreasonable, fascinating, absent-minded, amusing idler that ever bore the name of Herbert. Look him up and be amused', she advised her friend. I have looked him up, in an internet search combining their names, and discovered only that Herbert was honoured alongside Charles Dilke at the republican political meeting in 1872 attended by Eliza and her friend Mathilde Blind. If they were still in touch sixteen years later and on such friendly terms, I might have hoped to learn more, but no further information has appeared. Nor have I been able to find anything substantial about the connection with Mathilde Blind.

She apparently knew Richard Garnett, a scholar-librarian at the British Library, well enough for him to send her an article about economics, knowing that she would share his sophisticated disdain for the author and the views expressed. Eliza thanked him in friendly, familiar terms, telling Garnett the piece had 'afforded me much amusement'. She added a joke about the author's foolish exercise of 'popular logic': 'We are not to explain the Law of Supply & Demand because the phenomenon is as old as the Hills: ergo we are not to analyse air because Adam had lungs'. Their exchange happened in May 1873, around the time that she was starting to study with Savill Vaizey. I have searched in vain for further evidence of the Orme-Garnett connection and found nothing. As with the Alexander letters, it is only because Garnett's papers are preserved at the Harry Ransom Center in Texas that I got to know of their relationship.

Another friendship that can be documented with certainty is with Charles and Emilia Dilke, a Liberal politician and the remarkable woman who was his second wife. Eliza was braving a snowstorm when she went to St James's Hall with her friend Mathilde Blind to hear Sir Charles Dilke honoured at a huge political meeting as early as 1872. At that time he was already a Liberal Member of Parliament, a supporter of women's suffrage and other radical causes, whose name was mentioned as a future prime minister. Dilke's political leadership opportunities were blighted when he became involved in a very messy divorce scandal in 1885. (He had an affair with his brother's mother-in-law, and was accused of seducing a woman called Virginia Crawford who was a member of the lover's family; Dilke's court case went disastrously wrong and his reputation was badly damaged). That first letter from Eliza Orme to Samuel Alexander is almost certainly a reply to one from him, seeking advice about the Dilke case, although no names are mentioned. In the letter, she passionately asserts the politician's innocence and refers to her own 'strong personal liking' for the man, mentioning that she had 'been much concerned' in the case. The extent of Orme's 'concern', and what it means, will show up in Chapter 8. Meanwhile, you can read more about the scandal in Kali Israel's excellent book and article on the subject. Dilke's political career did recover enough for him to return to politics but not to become Prime Minister as some had hoped. In 1892 he ran as a Liberal candidate in the Forest of Dean constituency, and Eliza Orme was among his campaign workers.

Fig. 7 Sir Charles Wentworth Dilke, 2nd Bt. and Emilia Francis (née Strong), Lady Dilke (1894, W. & D. Downey, published by Cassell & Co. Ltd.), ©National Portrait Gallery, London.

Emilia Dilke's interests embraced the unlikely combination of trade unionism and art history. Among other occupations, she became leader of the Women's Trade Union League. Lady Dilke had a regular column in the *Women's Gazette and Weekly News*. In the case of the Dilkes, there is evidence of shared political and intellectual interests and of Eliza Orme's fierce loyalty in the face of scandal; there is also my suspicion (see Chapter 5) that Charles Dilke was a silent partner in the ownership of Orme's journalism project, the *Women's Gazette*. All of that is compelling, but the fact remains that I have found no evidence of the three friends writing to one another, and hence no evidence of the warmth (or otherwise) of their relationships.

Then there are people whose lives touched hers, who may or may not have been friends. One of these was Manomohan Ghose, who was the first practicing barrister of Indian origin. It may have been friendship that motivated her to edit a book in which he figured, or their relationship might have been more collegial, or even businesslike. Ghose was older than Orme, studying law at University College in the 1860s, so they were not fellow students though both were active in women's rights and other progressive circles before he went back to India. He did return to England briefly in 1885, so perhaps they encountered or reconnected with each other on that occasion; certainly they met in 1896 when she attended a public debate he was involved in. The book she edited, *The Trial of Shama Charan Pal: An Illustration of Village Life in Bengal*, featured a court case in which Ghose was the defending barrister. The book was published by Lawrence and Bullen in 1897, so it is also possible that the link with him was via the Lawrences. Whatever the motivation, the book is typical of Orme's energetic, practical approach to challenges, whether they related to career, domestic arrangements, or political life. The relationship, however, remains opaque.

The same goes for her ten-year friendship, if that is what it was, with George Gissing, one that extended for a further decade of contact with his estranged second wife and children. Although this relationship is quite well-documented, the surviving evidence comes from the perspective of the novelist, and he tended to be rather complacent about the practical and imaginative aid he received from that quarter. Gissing was the same age as Beatrice Orme, born in 1857. As a young man, his promising intellectual career had been cut short when he was imprisoned—and expelled from college—for stealing money with the objective of helping a troubled young woman with whom he was involved. (Nell Harrison was a working-class woman who had been engaged in sex work.) Their eventual marriage left him stuck in the lower middle class with a chip on his shoulder, a condition that he turned to brilliant use in the plots and characterization of his novels. By the time Gissing met Orme in 1894 he had married his second wife and they had a son. (Edith Underwood, too, was from the working classes and seems to have experienced some mental health challenges.) His novel *The Odd Women* had been out for about a year at this point. Gissing mentions in his diary that he has promised his publisher Henry Walton Lawrence of Lawrence and Bullen 'to dine with him and Bullen to meet Miss Orme shortly', but he gives no reason why this promise has been extracted or offered. The invitation duly arrived and Gissing acquired a dress suit, though he later realized he had not needed it. They dined at the Adelphi Restaurant and later went to the publishers' Henrietta Street offices to smoke and talk, 'Miss Orme taking a cigar as a matter of course'. At this point Orme was well-known in London, as the Senior Lady Assistant Commissioner on the recently completed Royal Commission investigation of labour conditions, but if Gissing knew that he was not impressed enough to mention it in his diary or in any of the surviving letters to friends. Around the same time Gissing was also building a friendship with one of Orme's colleagues on the Commission, Clara Collet.

Fig. 8 George Robert Gissing (1897, William Rothenstein), ©National Portrait Gallery, London.

Gissing must have stayed in touch with Orme because he turned for both practical and emotional support to both her and Collet when his marriage began to break down in 1897. By this time there was a second baby. Edith Gissing's side of the story remains undocumented, whereas the eloquent author wrote bitterly of her unacceptable behaviour and of his own unhappiness, both in a diary and in letters to friends. Most of his biographers seem to take Gissing's judgement of Edith at face value, but it is worth noting that Orme and Collet saw both sides of the dispute, at least initially. Perhaps they regarded Edith's outbursts as consistent with the extravagant rhetoric of the working-class women they had encountered in their labour investigations, rather than the evidence of insanity perceived by George Gissing. They both helped Gissing to manage his familial and legal obligations. ('What toil and misery she is taking off my hands', he wrote of Orme.) In September he agreed to pay Orme the considerable sum of £50 a quarter to care for Edith and the baby, Alfred, as lodgers in the home she shared with Beatrice and Charles Edward. Initially both she and Collet hoped to reconcile the couple, but by February of 1898, Orme found somewhere else for the mother and son to live, advised Gissing to seek a legal separation, and recommended her own solicitor. She found lodgings nearby for Edith and Alfred with 'a decent working-class woman who could let part of her house unfurnished'. Gissing recorded in August 1898 that Edith had 'written an insulting and threatening postcard' to Miss Orme, addressed 'Bad Eliza Orme'. Perhaps Edith felt betrayed.

Certainly there is a lot we do not know about all these relationships. The relentless scholarship of Gissing scholars like Michael Collie and Pierre Coustillas extends to peripheral people in the novelist's life, people like Orme and Collet, but only insofar as they fit into the scholar's analysis of the novelist's family situation. In the case of Coustillas, in particular, this analysis followed Gissing's own and was unsympathetic to Edith's perspective. Later, after Edith had been arrested and subsequently confined to a mental-health institution, Orme called upon her sister Blanche Fox to find a farming family in Cornwall who took care of Alfred; this cost Gissing a mere £19 per year.

When I wrote about Eliza Orme's career in terms of its precarity, for the 2021 essay collection *Precarious Professionals*, I speculated that the task of housing, feeding, and supervising Edith and Alfred Gissing might have been a paid gig—perhaps a welcome supplement to her income after the Royal Commission and the committee on prison conditions had ceased to provide any revenue. I realize there was more to the relationship between Orme and Gissing than a cash transaction, but I also believe the association was more complicated than Coustillas and other Gissing scholars have allowed. Knowing Orme as I now do, it seems obvious there was more to it than her endless kindness and sympathy for the genius of the tortured novelist. A tiny example: Coustillas has trouble understanding why Gissing might have received an invitation from the editor of the *Weekly Dispatch*, who contacted him in 1897 about an authorship opportunity. W. A. Hunter was editor of this newspaper for only five years; mostly he appears in reference works as a Liberal politician and law professor. As with Orme, Hunter's journalism work is less well known. The editor said he heard of Gissing through Mrs Ashton Dilke (a women's rights activist and his former student, the sister-in-law of Charles Dilke), but he may well have been concealing a closer connection: Eliza Orme wrote anonymous editorial essays (leaders) for the newspaper and she had known Hunter since her student days at University College. My guess is that she was either discreetly extending some practical help to Gissing as someone who needed a little cash, or else she was offering her editor a contact with a proven writer. Maybe even both. I wonder what she thought about Gissing's refusal to take up the offer, and his expressed concern that his artistic output would be 'tainted' by juxtaposition with the trashy sort of popular fiction that appeared in the *Weekly Dispatch*?

As with the Dilke couple, there is no way to recover the texture of the relationships between the two estranged Gissing spouses and Eliza Orme. To use that fraught term, there was a certain 'intimacy' to both friendships, because she knew things about both couples that were private. As well, the boundary between 'friend' and 'legal advisor' in both relationships may have got blurred when tensions were high. I wonder how she addressed George and Edith, or Charles and Emilia, in face-to-face conversation—and how she talked to Beatrice about them when the two sisters were alone?

With other acquaintances, there is often insufficient evidence even to speculate on the level of familiarity. Orme worked closely with Sophia Fry, Sophia Byles, Alice Westlake and others in the Women's Liberal

Federation, but it is difficult to know which of those people were friends and which merely colleagues. Sophia Bryant, however, does seem to have been a real friend. Bryant was always identified by her science degree (D.Sc.) in women's suffrage and Liberal publications, just as Orme was by her law degree. Bryant was from an Anglo-Irish family, and (like Eliza Orme) trained as a mathematician. She had been widowed at the age of twenty and used that independent social position to study mathematics and then make a name for herself both in her profession and in the Women's Liberal Federation and other feminist causes. But as with the Dilkes and so many others, the tone of the friendship is out of reach to us today.

Playing to the Gallery

It seems to me that the relationship of mentor and protégée was important to Eliza Orme, as was the collegial closeness that can develop between people working together on the same project or cause. In my own life I have benefitted immensely from being mentored by senior scholars, while becoming a mentor in my turn has been equally rewarding. Some of those relationships have turned into friendships, while others have faded a bit when we no longer see each other at academic gatherings. There is almost always a dynamic of unequal power in the relationship between two people who started out as mentor and protégé, though that dynamic does not always get acknowledged.

One protégée from early in Orme's career was Hertha Marks (better known in later life as the engineer/mathematician Hertha Ayrton). In one of her letters to Helen Taylor, in November 1875, Eliza mentioned that she had heard that Taylor 'would like to help a clever girl study at Girton'. The one she had in mind was about twenty, daughter of a Jewish widow in poor circumstances and encumbered with a younger sister. Orme herself had taught mathematics to Miss Marks, and the powerful women's movement leader Barbara Leigh Smith Bodichon was also interested in her case. Taylor did as she was asked, and Orme duly acknowledged a cheque for £25. I hope that, in helping Hertha Marks, Eliza understood how someone who lacked her own economic and familial privileges must be having a much more difficult time than she herself had experienced.

Later in life, just before her stint on the Royal Commission on Labour, Orme mentored Alice Ravenhill (1859–1954), later one of the first women to do public health inspection work, advising Ravenhill that 'There is such a thing as legitimate "playing to the gallery"'. In other words, it was a good idea to perform one's competence for the benefit of a powerful audience, and a bad idea to hide one's light under the proverbial bushel. She added that 'one should never lose an opportunity to see, hear, or if possible, secure contact—however momentary—with persons of note'. Finally, she recommended, a young woman with Ravenhill's kind of ambitions ought always to 'apply to the fountainhead for information'— that is, go directly to whoever held authority in a given situation. There is plenty of evidence that Eliza took her own advice as she built her own career, but it is delightful to know exactly how she articulated it for someone else.

Alice Ravenhill moved to Canada after establishing herself in England as a practitioner of home economics. In British Columbia she supported and advocated for Indigenous arts and crafts among other interests. Ravenhill's memories of Orme's advice turn up in her autobiographical writings. In addition to those published memoirs, a great many of Ravenhill's letters have been preserved in the British Columbia Archives, the University of British Columbia Library, and in Library and Archives Canada. These two women lived parallel lives in some ways (Ravenhill was born eleven years after Orme and she lived to be ninety-five), but the difference was that one's papers were mostly lost while the other's were, mostly, preserved for research.

Many of Orme's own mentors were male, the professors like Hunter and others who had taught her in university, the barristers like Phipson Beale who helped her get a foothold in Chancery Lane, and the politicians like John Stuart Mill whose aloof encouragement shaped some key moments of her career. Presumably she 'played to the gallery' with some of them, first in classrooms and then in the chambers of the Inns of Court, at Liberal Party gatherings, or in private meetings. In her appeal to Helen Taylor, she can be seen 'applying to the fountainhead for information', seeking moral as well as financial support and (perhaps) useful introductions. That was a complicated relationship, in that Taylor controlled Orme's access to Mill. In any case, it is pretty clear that relationship did not develop into a friendship; in fact it seems to have devolved into antagonism.

All of these people—parents, siblings, nephews and nieces, friends, lovers(?), acquaintances, protégées, colleagues—drifted in and out of Eliza's life over the decades of her education, political work, and quasi-professional career. As we will see, her public prominence peaked in the early 1890s when she was in her mid-forties but continued for another decade. The deaths of both her parents in 1893 may have precipitated a rethinking of priorities and possibilities. Charles Orme's will left everything to be divided among his three unmarried children, but Eliza was made executor of the estate. The three siblings moved from the Chiswick house to the new one (possibly newly built) in Tulse Hill not long after.

Who, then, was the private Eliza Orme? And whose was she—whose friend, colleague, antagonist, lover, lawyer, sister? Whose aunt or niece, editor or mentor? With all the sensational tidbits on Eliza Orme's private life that have surfaced for me recently, it has been more and more tempting to believe I know enough to reconstruct her life on the page, with authority and certainty. But I remain absolutely certain that I cannot, that much more information remains unrecovered, some lost forever and some waiting for the right questions to be asked, the right archives consulted. With respect to the question of her sexuality, for example, and remembering the need for discretion on the part of women in public life, it is possible that Eliza's relationship with Reina was strictly one of business and family friendship. Or that there was another woman, or perhaps a man, whose role in her life I will never know. I would not, after all, know about her and Sam Alexander if he had not happened to be a distinguished philosopher whose personal papers were preserved, organized, and documented by the university to which he devoted his career. But she and Sam were chums, more like cousins with a ten-year age gap to enhance the gender difference. Eliza and Reina were chums, too—girlfriends who also worked together on political campaigns and in their Chancery Lane chambers when they were not organizing parties where iced lemonade and bananas were served. Each of them had a life and a reputation in the public eye, but their correspondence, even if such letters ever survived the accidents of time, was not likely to receive the same archival attention as that of

Alexander or of Gissing. Not only that: both Eliza and Reina had a lot more to lose than did their male contemporaries. When scandal touched the life of the radical politician Charles Dilke, his career eventually recovered, whereas theirs would have been irretrievably damaged. In any case, I suppose both women believed that posterity had no business delving into their privacy.

Public life, however, was another matter. Like other extraordinary women of her time, Orme saw her achievements recorded as news items. She had the opportunity to express her views in published opinion pieces. And her adversaries were eager to record their opposition to her actions.

5. Public Figure:
1888 to about 1903

Beginning about the time of her law degree in 1888, the 'Miss Orme' who had been active in behind-the-scenes feminist and Liberal politics became a respected public figure, and sometimes a controversial one. Brief notices began to appear in the press, reporting on her drawing-room and public lectures and her rousing speeches at political meetings. Then on 3 March 1892, a full-fledged profile of Eliza Orme appeared in the *British Weekly*, a widely-circulated newspaper. The occasion was her appointment to lead an investigation, for a Royal Commission on Labour, into working conditions for women in several branches of British industry. There had been controversy about involving Lady Assistant Commissioners in the project, but the author assured readers that 'her presence guarantees the women's reports against sensationalism, the evidence against looseness and irrelevance'.

The article was anonymous (and indeed I am working from a reprint that appeared in another paper), but the author may have been the *British Weekly's* editor, William Robertson Nicoll. Whoever wrote the article must have known quite a lot about Orme, since they not only mentioned her family ('the early environment of a brilliant literary circle') but also noted her promising work in mathematics, her mentors, her law degree, and her practice of 'that part of the legal profession which is open to women in England'. Nicoll was in a position to know all that. The article praised Orme's powers as a debater and public speaker as it touched on her practical nature and propensity to crack a joke: 'Rhetoric and fine language are abhorrent to her. The pathos of facts seems to her more effective than that of mere words, and humour a healthier instrument, as a rule, for the handling of an audience than sentiment'. Establishing Orme's notoriety in the context of her

  https://doi.org/10.11647/OBP.0392.05

leadership of the Women's Liberal Federation, the article commented on a dispute then underway: 'in one section of the Federation, her name is one to conjure with; in another, it inspires horror and alarm'. In future she might be remembered as either 'a comet or the north wind'. The author went on to explain that for some women supporters of the Liberal Party, Miss Orme was an 'arch-villain', a 'malignant schemer ... whose every action is full of sinister meaning, to whom intrigue is both meat and drink, in whose "good morning" there is guile, and on whose lips the multiplication table would be full of undiscoverable, but none the less dangerous wickedness'. Whereas to her allies she was 'the quick-witted champion, with a convenient appetite for combat, at once capable and ready to be captain or scapegoat'. Beyond her brilliant rhetoric and political strategizing, Orme's friends identified 'a certain genial sympathy and helpfulness which they affirm to be peculiarly her own'.

What was this all about, and why did I know nothing about it until I started doing extensive research on the internet? Just as the letters archived at the University of Manchester have expanded my awareness of Eliza's 'genial sympathy and helpfulness' to Samuel Alexander, another recently recovered document helps me understand where the harsher characterizations were coming from. This time, however, the material is in print not manuscript, and I found it in a volume that might be unique in the whole world. A bulky volume of bound newspapers somehow avoided accessioning by the British Library, but nevertheless made its way from a political office in London to a university library in Eugene, Oregon. It was once the Women's Liberal Federation's own copy of the last few issues of the *Women's Gazette and Weekly News*, a paper that Orme edited for most of its history–until the Royal Commission appointment that occasioned her resignation and the *British Weekly* article.

Most profiles of Eliza Orme mention her membership in the Women's Liberal Federation and duly note that she, along with Catherine Gladstone and others associated with the male leaders of the party, broke away from the WLF in 1892 over the question of women's suffrage. This is a rather confusing and not very satisfactory bit of information. Her position can easily be misconstrued as a betrayal of the feminist cause, elitist, and generally on the wrong side of history.

Briefly, Orme's faction, the moderate majority, were determined that the issue of women's suffrage not be raised by the WLF in such a way as to embarrass or undermine William Ewart Gladstone's leadership of the party and in government. Her opponents in the 'progressive' faction were out-and-out suffragists, determined that the Federation should insist the party support their cause in the House of Commons, and prepared to undermine the organization in order to get their way. It is a complicated story, but everything becomes a good deal clearer with access to the volume in Eugene. In those pages lie the evidence for Orme's efforts to stave off the zeal of naïve political enthusiasts who did not, in her view, understand that they were putting their own (Liberal) cause at risk. Her efforts failed when it came to the women's branch of the party, as I shall explain, although she may have preserved her own reputation and standing with the broader Liberal leadership. Which would be remarkable, given the messiness of the situation that developed in the spring of 1892.

Eliza Orme was editor of the WLF's newspaper, the *Women's Gazette and Weekly News* (*WGWN*) from 1889 to 1892. I am not certain about how significant the role of editor was to her multifaceted identity: during the years she was an editor, she was also practicing as a quasi-lawyer; she belonged to numerous organizations that advocated various progressive causes; and she was on the board of a building society that offered mortgages. She was also an executive member and outspoken advocate for an auxiliary to the Liberal Party, the WLF. Her newspaper served as the WLF's 'organ' but was not formally associated with the Federation. This is another moment for the questions: who was she, and whose was she? My guess is that Orme regarded being an editor merely as one aspect of her leadership and advocacy—something useful that a 'hopelessly practical' supporter could do as a contribution to the cause. But which cause? She was ardently committed both to small-l-liberal ideas and to large-L-Liberal Party policy and strategy, as well as to the feminist aims of parliamentary suffrage, education, and work opportunities. Presumably she had all those interests in mind when she took on the job. But being an editor of a small, poorly funded, weekly national newspaper was not a nominal or honorary position. To read through the paper is to trace the evidence of Eliza Orme's intense involvement as a journalist, newsgatherer, opinion leader, production/ advertising manager, and finance officer.

As it happens, I have never yet read through the paper in the conventional way, which would have meant visiting the British Library and requesting the bound volumes containing the copies that institution owns, then sitting down in a reading room and turning over the pages, perhaps getting a little Victorian printer's ink on my fingers as I took notes on my laptop. I visited the BL often during my research career, first the original building in Bloomsbury and later the new one in St Pancras—both neighbourhoods in central London. I even went once or twice to Colindale, a far-northern suburb of London where the Newspaper Library used to be situated, but I was looking for different periodicals and never once thought of asking to see the *WGWN*. By the time I returned to researching Eliza Orme after 2014, I quickly discovered that the British Library's copies had been microfilmed, so that I could read them on a device at Robarts Library at the University of Toronto. I could even take digital scans of individual pages to facilitate my research. That was quite satisfying, and I learned a lot about Orme's lecturing and other activities, and something of the WLF as an organization. I also soon realized that the BL collection was incomplete. They have issues from the beginning in 1888 and through 1889. Then 1890 is missing, and only a few issues from 1891 are there. The standard reference works made no mention of any copies in existence, apart from those deposited—by law—in the British Library by the newspaper's publisher at the time of publication.

My friend Lorraine Janzen Kooistra, scholar of another branch of the Victorian periodical press, suggested I check WorldCat for further copies of the *WGWN*, a strategy that had worked for a colleague of hers looking for an obscure literary magazine. WorldCat is an online union catalogue, combining multiple library catalogues from around the world. WorldCat stated that the Special Collections Library of the University of Oregon at Eugene held copies of *WGWN* from 1890 to 1892. Once I got over my initial astonishment, I wrote to the librarians who sent a description of the materials—a single bound volume—and suggested a research assistant I might be able to hire to read it for me.

I also considered going to Eugene, a slightly daunting prospect for a woman in her seventies travelling alone with no idea how voluminous or useful the materials would be. First I corresponded with the freelance researcher the librarians had suggested, but that did not work out. Then I despaired for a while, and then 2020 and the Covid-19 pandemic came along. I returned to the Eugene website and this time discovered that they would digitally scan materials in their collection, for a fee. Unable to travel in any case, I was delighted to pay (about $C4000) for scans of each and every page of the Eugene volume and have access to them on my own computer.

Closer examination of the British Library Catalogue, and correspondence with their staff, revealed that their collection had initially included 1890 but that volume has been lost for many years. After 1888-89 there were a few issues from 1891, but the BL collection never, apparently, ever included the ten crucial issues covering the period January through November 1892. That is where the evidence unfolds of the conflict between Miss Orme and her allies on the one hand, and the 'Progressive Party' of the WLF on the other, the events that explain why her opponents regarded Eliza Orme as a malignant schemer to whom intrigue was meat and drink.

Before I get to the 'intrigue', however, I want to work chronologically through Eliza Orme's public life as we know it. This activity runs in parallel with her legal career through those years from 1875 to about 1903 when the various chambers in and around Chancery Lane were in operation and Orme and her partners prepared property documents for barristers and solicitors, managed patent applications, and engaged in the loan operations of a building society. First there was her public engagement with various political and social causes, notably that of Home Rule for Ireland. Then her involvement with the WLF and the Federation's split over the question of women's suffrage as Liberal Party policy. Next I will discuss the Royal Commission on Labour and the role of factory inspector, as well as her appointment to a committee investigating conditions in women's prisons. In the following chapter, I turn to Eliza Orme's journalism as another aspect of her public life – not just the *Women's Gazette* but her authorship of books and articles in several different venues.

Public Engagement and the Campaign for Irish Home Rule

From very early adulthood, Eliza Orme was eager to take on leadership positions in organizations devoted to the causes she thought were important and to write about those causes for mainstream periodicals. I mentioned in Chapter 3 that John Stuart Mill manoeuvred her onto the London Committee for Women's Suffrage executive in 1871 when she was only twenty-two years of age, having just abandoned her mathematical studies in favour of law. The following year found Eliza attending, with her friend Mathilde Blind, a republican meeting honouring the radical politicians Charles Dilke and Auberon Herbert. In 1874, now twenty-five, she wrote a couple of articles for *The Examiner* about the fraught question of University degrees for women. That periodical also published her acerbic article, 'Sound-Minded Women' the same year, and a poem ('Song') in 1875. She taught a short course on the elements of law for the North London Collegiate School. (I learned this from Anne Bridger's doctoral thesis). She attended meetings of the Association for the Promotion of the Legal Education of Women and later, with her partner Mary Ellen Richardson, joined that Association's Executive Committee. She joined a Ladies' Debating Club and later the Women's Political League. She was involved in the 1878 foundation of the Somerville Club for women—a somewhat contentious occasion that I still have not got to the bottom of, although it was apparently at her instigation that the Club later refused to accept the daughters of Charles Bradlaugh as members. In 1880, she gave the first of several addresses to the Sunday Lecture Society, on 'Free Trade in Education' and one to the Personal Liberty Club on 'The Evils of Compulsory Education'. Later (in May 1882) the Sunday Lecture Society heard her views on 'What shall we do with our criminal & neglected children' and the following year on 'Religious liberty. Do we possess it in England?' 1880 is the first record I have of a pro-women's suffrage lecture, but many more followed. Some were in public places like St. James's Hall; others were at drawing-room meetings in middle-class private homes. Others, remarkably, were at fortnightly sewing meetings held in a dissenting chapel, where women metal workers appeared with infants in arms to talk politics.

As Honorary Secretary of the newly-founded Women's Political League, in mid-1885, Orme spoke about the organization's objectives: to get women in general more interested in public affairs, to put them to work as canvassers for parliamentary candidates, and to see to it that capable women were elected to the executive councils of political associations. When challenged by someone who objected to women offering their services to candidates on record as opposed to women's suffrage, she replied: 'What would be more likely to bring about a general recognition of women's full rights as citizens than the fact that they were both able and willing to work side by side with men in public affairs?'. This was a robust point of view, but Orme was to learn that many of the feminist politicians of her generation did not share it.

All this activity attracted notice, of course, especially when it was observed alongside Orme's professional work providing legal services from chambers in Chancery Lane. Jealous fellow-students (like Pascoe Daphne) and sniping reporters (like the commentator in the *Sporting Gazette*) were ready to draw public attention to the anomaly of a single woman in public life. Private comments could be even more vicious: the aptly-named Miss E. M. A. Savage wrote to the novelist Samuel Butler in 1880 about an 'obnoxious article' written by Miss Orme on the subject of the new Somerville Club and took the opportunity to tell him she was 'happy to say that she is horribly ugly'. The thing is, there must have been dozens of other occasions—of everything from annoyance or sabotage to sniping or outright harassment—for every one that surfaces however slightly in the public record. Orme's calm demeanour and 'practical' approach to challenges must have concealed a great deal of frustration and distress. Still, the attention could sometimes be positive, as well as negative. Her political activity, and the convictions behind it, sometimes drew the attention of prominent men who were in a position to create opportunities for such a woman.

Several of Eliza Orme's interests still seem remarkably relevant in the twenty-first century. She belonged to the Proportional Representation Society. She took an interest in building a tunnel under the English Channel. She was a pacifist, belonging to the Arbitration and Peace Association. Certainly she was a strong supporter of women's rights, especially the right to work unimpeded in a chosen job or career. Her most passionate interest, however, the cause of Home Rule for Ireland, was a campaign whose objectives were realized in her lifetime, albeit not in the way she would have wanted or expected.

In the nineteenth century, the UK was called a 'united' kingdom because parallel acts of the British and Irish Parliaments (the Act of Union of 1800) had merged England, Wales, and Scotland with the Kingdom of Ireland. (Today's union includes only a small portion of the northern part of the island of Ireland, but then it was the whole country.) By the 1870s when Eliza Orme was coming of age politically, there was a strong movement within Ireland for 'home rule' (that is, for self-government) and a lot of support for the idea in England, too. The history of injustice and colonial rule was centuries-long and painful, but at this point it was the laws governing land ownership that caused the most hardship. Home rule would have to be 'granted' to Ireland by the British Parliament passing the necessary legislation. The idea appealed ideologically to many members of the Liberal Party in England, but others were adamantly opposed. From the mid-1880s to the mid-1890s, the issue divided the Liberals. In 1886 the Liberal Prime Minister, William Ewart Gladstone, introduced legislation that failed and split his party. The foundation of the Women's Liberal Federation the following year was, in part, a project of the Home Rule faction—with Sophia Fry and Catherine Gladstone at the forefront and Eliza Orme in the background, organizing and strategizing.

I do not know exactly what made Orme such a strong supporter of Home Rule, but I suspect that she absorbed the ideology from her university mentors and perhaps from some in her family circle. Home Rule was the issue that encapsulated calls for justice in her time—like the anti-Vietnam-war movement in my youth, or Black Lives Matter in the 2020s. She spoke and wrote enthusiastically about the cause. She also visited Ireland and came home to share her experiences with friends and with Liberal audiences. After one such trip, she wrote to Sam Alexander: 'We have got little peeps into the homes and the habits of the people which no reading—not even good novels—can give you and just now when the whole world is watching the Irish fight it is so exciting to feel one is getting hold of the real facts'. And a few lines later: 'Nothing I can say conveys a hundredth part of the worth of these people. We ought to begin to pay our debts to them pretty quickly for we are in monstrous arrears'.

She was eloquent, witty, and persuasive, not only in a private letter, but on the platform and in the committee room, and also on the pages of her weekly newspaper.

The *Women's Gazette* began in November 1888—initially as an independent periodical under a male editor, Sydney Hallifax, himself a prominent Home Ruler. From the beginning, however, Hallifax proclaimed the *Gazette* to be 'devoted to the social well-being and political education of women, with a chronicle of the work of the Women's Liberal Association'. The first issue featured an admiring profile of Mrs Gladstone and a clear statement that the newspaper would address the prominent question of the government of Ireland. Hallifax was editor, but it is not clear who was the newspaper's proprietor. After only a few weeks, an editorial statement attempted to quash a rumour that the newspaper was funded by none other than Charles Dilke, another Gladstonian and Home Rule supporter. (My suspicion is that Dilke was indeed backing the paper but everyone concerned preferred that he do so anonymously because of his divisive reputation.) Eliza Orme herself may well have been involved behind the scenes of the paper from the beginning, though I have found no evidence to that effect. She was announced as its editor and manager in September 1889, at the same time as ownership passed from Hallifax to a new company complete with shareholders and a board of directors, the Women's Gazette Printing & Publishing Company, Limited. Letters to that company were directed to Orme's chambers, and cheques were made out in her name, but as editor she undertook to report on Liberal women's meetings. In the WLF and the *Women's Gazette*, the Home Rule movement had an organization—and an organ—made up of supportive women eager to be politically active.

I have written about the *Women's Gazette* in a 2022 article for the *Victorian Periodicals Review*, because the newspaper is interesting for its own sake and because I wanted to publicize my uncovering those missing copies in the library in Oregon. Orme was its editor for most of the newspaper's four-year run. Hallifax, her predecessor, retired gracefully in her favour; and her successor, Eliza Brabrook, acted as a caretaker for the few issues that appeared after she left to work on the Royal Commission. Both of those people were political allies in Home Rule Liberal and other causes. In this book, however, I am using the

Gazette as a historical source for documenting Eliza Orme's public engagement, and especially her fraught engagement with the movement for women's suffrage.

The Women's Liberal Federation Splits over the Question of Suffrage

The matter of women's right to vote in Parliamentary elections had been prominent since the 1860s, and Eliza Orme was involved with the National Society for Women's Suffrage since attending meetings with her mother as a teenager. For her, it was an important issue, although not as urgent as Home Rule for Ireland. Orme's priorities were shared by the co-founders of the Women's Liberal Foundation and by Sydney Hallifax, the first editor of the *Women's Gazette*. All these Liberals were thinking strategically, taking into consideration the interests of their party, the unlikelihood of any particular bill being passed in both the House of Commons and House of Lords, and the desirability of enlisting support from people who opposed them on one issue while agreeing with them on another. It was practical politics. The flagship issue of the *Gazette* proclaimed; 'The most prominent question at the present time ... is, of course, the government of Ireland, and many thousands of Englishwomen, filled with deep sympathy for the sorrows of that unhappy country, are anxious so to direct their efforts as to secure the greatest possible results for good'. The editorial went on to admit that 'There is also a large group of political questions about which Liberals do not agree, and in which women are particularly interested'. A 'fair example' was the political enfranchisement of women. These questions would be discussed in the *Gazette's* columns with a 'perfectly impartial opening' available to both sides.

Neutrality with respect to women's suffrage lasted, as settled policy of the Women's Liberal Federation, only a little over two years. Early in 1890, Rosalind Howard, Countess of Carlisle, got involved and began to press for change. She told the annual meeting of the WLF Council in London that 'her heart was enflamed for women's suffrage' and noted that unlike 'Miss Orme, who has been supporting women's suffrage since 1866' she herself had only recently been 'allowed to go on the platform'. Lady Carlisle was unlike Miss Orme in most ways: not only a few years older, but born into a patrician rural family, educated at home, and married since the age of nineteen to a wealthy aristocrat and politician. (One of their properties was Castle Howard, which I have visited but remember best as the setting for the TV version of *Brideshead Revisited*.) Rosalind is recalled as 'the radical countess': she campaigned vigorously for abstention from alcohol, non-adulteration of food, and similar causes. She believed so strongly in Home Rule that she disagreed publicly with her husband on the issue; but even Home Rule was less important to her than votes for women. Lady Carlisle set about trying to persuade the leadership of the WLF to insist that women's suffrage become Liberal Party policy. This would have been an embarrassment and an impediment to Gladstone and the leadership, and reason enough for Orme and her allies to stand firm on the policy of neutrality.

Fig. 9   Rosalind Frances (née Stanley), Countess of Carlisle (1900s, H. Walter Barnett), ©National Portrait Gallery, London.

The pages of the *Women's Gazette* document the increasing acrimony within the Federation, and the use of underhanded tactics on the part of Lady Carlisle and her faction. These included manipulating ('beguiling') the politically naïve leaders of local Women's Liberal Associations in rural towns and villages—not necessarily to persuade them to support the cause, but to appoint proxy voters to the meetings of the central WLF Council (voters who would then cast ballots for the 'progressive' faction) or even to produce unauthorized ('counterfeit') affiliation forms with the purpose of swamping Council meetings with votes for their side. Both sides described this kind of politicking as 'wire pulling'. The volumes held in the British Library finish at the end of 1891, with Lady Carlisle referring to 'the divided state of the Federation' and Miss Orme speaking at a Nottingham meeting where resolutions were made concerning the great importance of female representation on the Labour Commission then being set up.

January 1892 initiated not just a new year but a new volume of the *WGWN*, the one to be found only in Eugene. With a digital copy in hand, I can report that conflict quickly escalated and recriminations abounded. Moderate members wondered whether Lady Carlisle and her 'Progressive Party' were aiming to make the WLF a single-issue organization, 'a fourth Suffrage Society'. They seemed to wish 'to carry the Council by storm'—influencing agents, forging the official affiliation forms, collecting money subscriptions, scheduling lectures free of expense to the local organizers, and similar tactics. An editorial observed that 'The "Progressive Party" is singularly unfortunate in its name. It is not progressive in any Liberal sense, and it is not a party'.

Eliza Orme and her allies knew something that Lady Carlisle and her faction overlooked: women's issues and women's politics were not limited to the suffrage question, and certainly not to in-fighting within one party's auxiliary. In particular, labour conditions for women working in industry were of vital importance. A news item of 8 February 1892 announced that 'The committee dealing with textile industries on Tuesday last came to the decision to recommend the appointment of Miss Orme, Miss Collett, Miss Abraham, and Miss Irwin as Sub-Commissioners to investigate the problem with regard to women's labour'. This was an event of huge importance to reforming politicians of all parties and of both sexes, but it mattered little to those 'progressives' among women Liberals who continued to see Orme as a 'malignant schemer' and an impediment to their single-issue objective. In the two months between that announcement and Orme's resignation from both the WLF executive and the newspaper editorship in early April, the chaos continued. Mary Martin Leake, the paid secretary who was loyal to the moderate leadership, reported 'difficulties introduced into the Federation office by an irreconcilable and irresponsible minority'. At one point one of the leadership had to implore Lady Carlisle not to insult Miss Leake. Somebody else observed that the WLF was 'like a bear garden', although it got worse after Orme's departure. The 'progressive' (suffrage as party policy now) minority refused to accept that their program, to which they were so passionately committed, would always be outvoted by the moderate (wait until later) majority. To the minority, dirty tricks seemed to be necessary in those circumstances.

Eliza Orme took on an influential and demanding full-time political position when she was appointed Senior Lady Assistant Commissioner, and the job required her to maintain a stance of objectivity. She was thus perfectly justified in resigning from both the Federation executive and the *Women's Gazette* editorship. Still, I cannot help wondering if Eliza regarded the new post as a sort of exit strategy—a means to get away from the distasteful and futile squabbles that had begun to take up so much of her time and energy. She was gone when some of the 'progressives' took possession of the WLF offices, locking themselves in and refusing admittance to the temporary secretary who replaced Mary Martin Leake. She was gone when the story, embellished and sensationalized, made its way into the mainstream press (were cheques and postal orders and even £90 in cash left lying around, or was that account 'untrue'?). At the newspaper office, her place was taken by Eliza Brabrook, a subeditor at Lawrence and Bullen, the publishing house co-owned by Reina Lawrence's brother Henry. Brabrook brought the newspaper to a decorous close after a further five issues, although she seems to have neglected to deposit the year's volume in the British Library.

As for the Federation, Orme and her colleagues resigned *en masse* from the leadership and later formed a Women's National Liberal Association, splitting the party's women's auxiliary with predictable results. Not only was a cadre of canvassers and other political workers unavailable to the party's candidates, but a fragile structure within which women could learn the skills of organization and public speaking was damaged. Both had been among Eliza Orme's 'practical' objectives for supporting the Women's Liberal Federation and its local Associations by editing its newspaper.

The early months of 1892 may also have signalled a change in Eliza's business address and professional practice. For the last year or two, press advertisements for the Nineteenth Century Building Society and editorial notices about the *WGWN* had given her address as 5 Dane's Inn, near Chancery Lane like the Southampton Buildings chambers she had for about eight years before that. I do not know exactly when she moved, but by September the NCBS was listing her address as 16 Henrietta Street. That was the address where Lawrence and Bullen had their publishing house, and it was in Covent Garden not in the legal district. It was also the address from which Eliza Brabrook published the final issues of the *WGWN*. Perhaps the two Elizas shared the same chambers, possibly on their own or possibly a set of rooms inside Reina's brother's place of business. On her new adventure, Miss Orme was not only going to be on the road and occupied with interviews, supervision, and report-writing, she need not be available to high-powered barristers needing assistance with complex property transactions.

Factory Inspection and the Royal Commission

Eliza Orme spent about eighteen months on the work of the Royal Commission, from January 1892 to June 1893. She was paid £25 (which translates to almost £4000 in modern money) per month. That was £5 more per month than her three colleagues, because she was the Senior Lady Assistant Commissioner and had to supervise their investigations and co-sign their reports. It was not a straightforwardly political appointment; in fact the government of the day was a Conservative one, although both Liberal and Labour politicians, as well as people concerned about the unhealthy conditions in many factories and workshops had been agitating on the subject for some time. She seems to have got the job through her old mentor Leonard Courtney, who was entrusted with the task of finding four suitable women. Courtney did not select Beatrice Potter, just about to marry Sidney Webb and now an avowed socialist; he did, however, tell Potter on January 4th that Orme and the others had been commissioned. From the Webbs' point of view, the report on women's work was only a sidebar to the Royal Commission on Labour that had been set up after a contentious strike at the London docks and focused on male labour and questions of trade unionism. But it was of vital importance to people on both sides of the question about women's work, those like Orme who wanted women to work unencumbered by regulation and those who sought to regulate labour in order to protect fragile female bodies. The news of the investigations hit the press late in February. March 7th 1892 marked both the first official meeting of the four Lady Assistant Commissioners with the civil servant who oversaw their work, and the last issue of the *Women's Gazette* to be edited by Miss Orme. She had a new and formidable challenge ahead of her.

The four members of the Royal Commission charged with investigating the employment of women had three broad tasks: tracking differences in the rates of wage of women versus men; looking into the 'alleged grievances of women'; and reporting on the effects of industrial employment on women's health, morality, and homes. They were particularly instructed to investigate the exclusion of women from certain trades. They could draw upon written information in existing government reports, but they were also adjured to visit 'centres of industry' and take evidence directly from both employers and employees. Each of the several reports to the Commission was to be signed by at least two of the Assistant Commissioners—in practice, by Eliza Orme and one of her subordinates. They were expressly committed to avoid expressions of personal opinion as to proposed legislation on these matters, and generally to stick to the facts. (This proved difficult for two of them, as it happens.) Clara Collet reported on working conditions in numerous industries in London, and also made a few forays to other urban centres. May Abraham's remit was the textile factories of the north and the Midlands, and the white lead industry in the north (with a few extra fields of work thrown in). Alongside Eliza Orme, Abraham also travelled to Ireland to report on women's work there. Margaret Irwin's job was also based geographically, this time in Scotland, where she looked particularly, but not exclusively, at the textile industries. Finally, Orme was assigned two further investigations: first the conditions of work for barmaids and others whose labour involved serving refreshments; and second the working conditions of women in the nail, chain and bolt-making industries in the Black Country (the coal fields of the West Midlands).

In her report on the work of barmaids, Orme reports that she spoke to 287 persons—127 women currently or formerly employed in bars and pubs, twenty-one women and eighty-nine men in the position of employers or superintendents, and a further fifty people who knew the customs of the trade. She visited ninety-one public houses, hotels and restaurants, twenty railway, theatre, and music hall bars, as well as forty-three places of refreshment not licensed to sell intoxicating liquors. Then there were visits to six residential institutions 'for the benefit of working girls' two of which were specially designed to provide accommodation for barmaids. That was a formidable amount of preparation, interviewing, data collection, and information management. The investigation took place in London, large towns in the south of England, the north of England, in Scotland and in Ireland. Orme's report is both detailed and dispassionate. She refers to specific individuals and their concerns. She reports mistreatment when she finds it, but she is careful to be respectful to employers and sceptical of the complaints of employees. Addressing a concern felt by some social reformers, she refutes concerns that bartending would lead either to drunkenness or overfamiliarity on the part of women workers. Later, she even became a vice-president of the Barmaids Political Defence League.

The report on women's work in Ireland is similarly aloof, noticeably lacking the partisan commitment to the Irish people that is evident in Orme's political rhetoric on the subject of Home Rule. For example she notes that 'the houses occupied by shop assistants in Ireland are often untidy and furnished in a very slovenly manner, but the essentials of comfort are not disregarded' and the accommodations compare favourably with those in England and Wales. She reports quite nonchalantly about the conditions of work in convent industries, the infamous Magdalene Homes, now better known as the Magdalene 'Laundries'. Here her focus was on the high quality of the laundry equipment, not on the practice of 'penitents' (unmarried mothers) being put to work on the premises where they were receiving prenatal care. When it came to the question of married women labourers and childcare—or rather, the lack of childcare—she made it clear that the women themselves were generally opposed to being kept away from work for as long as three months after childbirth.

The same observation appeared in Orme's report on women's work in the Black Country metalwork industries, specifically the manufacture of nails, chains, and bolts in both domestic workshops and small factories. For some reason this report does not appear with the others on women's employment. It came out earlier and was included as an appendix to the minutes of evidence taken on work in the metal trades generally. She visited Birmingham in May of 1892, seeing twenty-three different workplaces and interviewing employers, workers, and trades union leaders; her report was dated 21 June. The tone of this report is somewhat more opinionated than the others. Orme makes it clear that the women wanted to work, needed the income to support their families. Indeed, they would undoubtedly respond to any legislation preventing married women's work by 'avoiding the legal ceremony of marriage' and continuing to work at the forge, live common law in their parents' home, and have babies alongside their own mothers. But she took time to note that the nearest approach to 'common action' was not a union meeting but large attendance at a cookery class: 'This may seem to have no relation to trade combination, but the very earliest step towards combination, that of creating some kind of public spirit, has yet to be taken among these women, and a cookery class, which will give them a higher standard of home comfort, and at the same time draw them together, is perhaps the best way of beginning'.

Her final remarks to those who commissioned her investigation are classic Eliza Orme: sensible, pragmatic, acerbic, always practical:

> I cannot close this report without recording my astonishment at the unsuitable dress worn by these workers. Instead of a short skirt with a leathern apron to guard them from the edge of the forge, comfortable broad soled shoes without heels, and a loose cool jacket, they wear the worn-out Sunday frock, ragged, burned and heat-stained, tight stays, high heeled shoes, and a bit of sacking pinned over the skirt completing the untidiness. When they are hot they loosen the throat of the dress, and this increases the unseemliness of their general appearance. A class for teaching the simple rules of health, and a supply of suitable garments at cost price, are schemes well worth the attention of kind-hearted ladies who wish to better the condition of the women in the Black Country.

Lady Carlisle and similar 'kind-hearted ladies' would have ignored the practicalities of cookery lessons and a clothing allowance in favour of prohibiting paid work in such a rough industry altogether. Eliza Orme knew all too well the consequences of such an apparently kind-hearted policy, in the shape of hunger, malnutrition, and family violence. And neither of them could imagine a regime that might sponsor childcare services or support workplace safety regulations for people of all genders.

It is difficult to get a sense of the daily routine of her work on the Royal Commission. Eliza seems to have taken the hundreds of interviews in her stride, but perhaps that was a challenge. Certainly note-taking and reporting were skills she had to learn. (She did learn, and later advised a subordinate, Lucy Deane, 'not to buy smart leather bound note books, but soft cheap 3*d* school exercise books and indelible pencils; to keep one in her private handbag at all times, and to write immediately after any meeting, in cabs, hotels, trains, factories; and to keep a record of everyone and everything and everywhere she travelled; and to record her opinions and descriptions of everyone she met'.) For at least one of the investigations, the one in the Black Country, she travelled with a 'lady shorthand writer' who took charge of the notetaking.

I find myself comparing this to my own experience of a challenging but precarious new job when I began to teach history students at the University of Windsor while commuting back and forth to Toronto at weekends. I imagine that, for her, the travel must have been exhausting, though perhaps also exhilarating. And perhaps, too, we shared an optimism that was also ambition. Maybe she hoped that this eighteen-month gig would lead to better things, longer-lasting opportunities, a chance to make a name for herself in politics.

That is speculation, but I am on firmer ground in being able to puncture the seriousness of the reports, a bit, by quoting a letter from Eliza to Sam, dated from the Imperial Hotel in Cork on 12 November 1892. 'Here I am trying to find industries to report upon in Ireland. My old friends are very anxious to help but, alas, the subject of the enquiry is wanting. I shall have to pad my report with a little history and it won't do any harm'. Then she went on to tell him a funny story about an old man who made her laugh, and about how 'Dublin is looking very quiet and dignified in the autumn lights. The public buildings are so suitable and consistent I fall in love with them afresh each time I come'. The investigation was a good gig, a promising opportunity, but it was not her whole life.

There are numerous articles in the newspaper and periodical press about the reports of the Royal Commission, most of them unimpeachably straightforward and rather dull. One exception is an anonymous bit of doggerel in *Punch*, the famous comic magazine, published on 18 November 1893 with the tagline 'See the Report of the Lady Commissioners on Women's Labour'. The title, 'To Hebe' refers to a Greek goddess, sometimes described as the cupbearer to the gods, who was associated with youthful femininity and, by extension, with barmaids.

> To Hebe:
> Waitress with the dimpled chin,
> Cap as clean as a new pin,
> Here's a feather to put in!
>
> For Miss Orme's report declares
> That no male with you compares
> In the showing off of wares.
>
> Be it counter, be it bar,
> You can 'dress' it – you're its star,
> Bright, and most particular!
>
> Grievances you have, no doubt:
> Which of us exists without?
> Still, you do not pine or pout.
>
> Standing with reluctant feet
> Always ready, trim, and neat,
> No one tells you – 'Take a seat!'
>
> Hours are long, and meal-time short,
> Mashing bores, who think it 'sport',
> Say the things they didn't ought!
>
> Gather, then, the tips that fall;
> Don't let vulgar chaff appal;
> To the Bar you've had your 'call!'

Fortunately the anonymity of the author has been unveiled by the researchers behind the *Curran Index to Victorian Periodicals*. He was a lawyer, a barrister, and a sometime novelist, Horace Frank Lester (1853–1896). Lester must have enjoyed writing that last double-meaning line, but I do not suppose Eliza Orme enjoyed reading it.

One reader of *Royal Commission on Labour: the Employment of Women* was distinctly enthusiastic. A young David Lloyd George, then a new Member of Parliament for a Welsh constituency (and much later Britain's Prime Minister) wrote a letter to his brother in which he zeroed in on the parts of Orme's report that referred to women's work in Wales: 'What a squasher. Tremendous. Ellis & I sat down for an hour to meditate upon it & chew it like a "joy o bacco" & spit it out'. For politicians of a progressive stripe, this report provided plenty to chew on.

A more measured response came in a review that appeared in *The Economic Journal* (in March 1894, by Caroline A. Foley). It sums up the general tone of the reports on women's labour, reveals that two of the lady assistant commissioners ignored the stipulation that they avoid expressing opinions, and comments on their personalities. 'There is literary interest', Foley noted, 'in watching the methods and standpoints of the several authors:–the disinterested, manysided watchfulness and statistical skill of Miss Collet, the championship of the worker and her wrongs throbbing through Miss Abraham's columns; the sagacious conclusions and sympathetic insight of Miss Irwin, whose Scotch lassies with "the bit shawlie" over their heads we seem to know personally; and the judicial balancing of evidence evinced by Miss Orme's legal culture'. Collet, it seems, thought like a sociologist and social worker, and Orme like a lawyer. Whereas both Abraham and Irwin were unabashedly in sympathy with the women whose working conditions they were commissioned to interrogate.

There is some evidence that the 'judicial' Miss Orme had to use her 'legal culture' and experience to rein in the passionate enthusiasms of both Abraham and Irwin. In the case of Irwin, the Aberdeen Trades Council suspected that Orme had suppressed evidence in the course of 'compiling' Irwin's report and this concern was reported in the press. Two Members of Parliament wrote letters to the editor of the *Aberdeen Evening Express* (7 December 1893). One attested to Orme's 'eminent competence' (this was James Bryce who, with his wife, worked with Orme on Liberal and Home Rule issues). The other affirmed that 'Miss Orme is usually considered very trustworthy' (this was W. A. Hunter,

M.P. and not the first time he had advocated for her.) Eliza Orme was not the Conservative lackey that the Labour Party of Aberdeen imagined her to be, but she did understand her responsibility to ensure that the tone of the reports had to be as neutral as possible if they were to be well-received. And she was, after all, an editor—well versed in revising someone else's prose for publication in print.

Beginning in 1893, immediately after the Royal Commission, the Liberal government then in power appointed a number of women as paid factory inspectors, specifically to examine and report on working conditions for women on an ongoing basis. Eliza Orme was not one of them. It seems clear to me that she was not interested in that sort of employment, although it would be nice to know if it was offered to her. At least one of her three lady-assistant-commissioner colleagues, May Abraham (later Tennant) was hired and began a lifelong distinguished career in this kind of work. Another of the initial intake of women inspectors was Lucy Deane, whom Eliza Orme had advised about notetaking. Deane remembered Orme's warning that if she took the position, she would have to be careful to avoid partisanship, whether with a political party or a trade union. Eliza Orme took her own advice a couple of years later, when she joined a committee to investigate the conditions in prisons.

Prison Committee

Early in 1894 there was an outcry in the daily press about the conditions in prisons and the treatment of prisoners. William Gladstone's Liberal government responded by setting up a committee on the matter, chaired by his son, Herbert Gladstone. Eliza Orme was the only woman on the committee, which began its investigations that summer and reported in April 1895. I do not know whether this one was a paid assignment, although I suspect so. Orme asked questions of the people testifying to the committee and joined her colleagues in signing the resulting report. Most of her concern appears to have been for the women who staffed the prisons as warders, rather than for the benighted prisoners themselves—at least on the surface. The author of a 1994 book on the contemporary prison system, Sean McConville, regards her contribution as 'surprisingly pusillanimous', noting that Orme felt strongly about the charity workers who came into prisons and interfered with their operation by professional managers. She also, for some reason McConville could not understand, made a considerable fuss about insisting that women prisoners should not be allowed to cook food that was intended for consumption by women warders. Pusillanimous or not she maintained her reputation for practicality, recommending that it would be best for women to be assigned prison labour that would prepare them for jobs they could secure once they were released. When the report appeared, newspapers referred to Orme as 'a lady whose name is a household word with all who take interest in the question of prison reform'.

Four years after the Committee's official report, with a Prisons Bill in front of Parliament at the time of publication, Eliza Orme wrote a brief signed article for the *Fortnightly Review* entitled 'Our Female Criminals'. Among other things, the article answers McConville's question about prisoners cooking for warders. The article did not refer directly to her own authorship of the recommendations it cited, too many of which had been 'quietly ignored'. The article was unabashedly feminist ('The fact is that our prison administration is entirely in the hands of men, and partly from ignorance of the wants and characteristics of women, and partly from fear of doing more harm than good, the Commissioners [of prisons] turn a deaf ear to suggestions of radical reform. The matrons are often clever, experienced women, but, like most salaried officials, they know it is their wisest policy to obey orders without making suggestions'.) The five-page article goes on to make numerous recommendations, most of which had already appeared in Orme's official report. Drunkenness was a problem; so were prison labour, diet, and exercise, the care of mothers incarcerated with nursing infants, spiritual guidance, and job training. And here we find an explanation of Orme's concern with prisoners, themselves 'on a strict diet', being assigned to cook meals for the warders: 'A woman who has not tasted tea for six months has to pour the boiling water on the fragrant leaf, and is punished when a few tea leaves are found concealed in her pocket. She is living on brown bread and the prison broth, and she is expected to fry sausages without pilfering'. Despite this imaginative sensitivity to inmates, Orme is again eloquent on the needs of the prison matrons: she evokes the domestic comfort of a male warder who has a home and family to spend time with off duty, whereas his female counterpart either shares accommodation with other matrons on the prison grounds, perpetually 'talking prison gossip and prison grievances over the fire in their common sitting-room', or languishes 'in her lonely little home'. Under such conditions, it was rare to find women prison staff of the kind Eliza Orme admired: 'with sunny tempers, bright hopeful spirits, and bubbling over with originality'.

Unlike the Royal Commission on Labour, I have not found evidence of a continuing interest on Orme's part in prison reform. The committee's investigations, the report, and the later *Fortnightly Review* article do, however, constitute her final foray into public life as this chapter has conceptualized it.

An Independent Single Professional Woman in Public Life

All this activity in the public-facing part of Eliza Orme's life in the 1880s and 90s makes it hard to understand how she came to remain quite unknown to posterity for such a long time, and why she is still relatively obscure. Part of the answer lies in the pivotal year of 1892. Eliza was forty-three that year (turned forty-four on Christmas day). Her legal career had, perforce, been so tightly restricted that it had not generated much of a reputation, although she was valued in her professional capacity by the handful of barristers who employed her services. She was the head of her own household. Her political activity and ambitions had been diverted from the Liberal Party's big issues (especially Home Rule for Ireland) to the party's women's auxiliary. Here she did her best to organize and educate her fellow members as well as her leadership colleagues. But now the Royal Commission might offer the opportunity to sit at the same table with powerful male colleagues and have her voice heard and respected. Instead, she was drawn into a dispute among women that many men found laughable, while many women chose the opposite side. In the Countess of Carlisle and her allies, Eliza came up against a feminism very different from her own, a feminism more emotional than intellectual, more idealistic than strategic. The encounter put her on the wrong side of history. Lady Carlisle's feminism was associated with a campaign whose extraordinary struggle, eventual success, and evident justice have made it difficult for people in the twentieth and twenty-first centuries to see that 'votes for women' might have come about any other way. This is not the place to discuss whether there might have been another way, but rather to think about why Eliza Orme's public life did not generate the kind of memorial narrative it might have otherwise. One reason is that her reputation turned out to be collateral damage in Carlisle's mission to make the Women's Liberal Federation over as a suffragist organization. That mission was a small part of the 'radical Countess's' activities, but it may have put an irreparable barrier in the way of Eliza Orme's path to significant political influence.

Another reason was longevity: she was only halfway through her lifespan in 1892. By the time Eliza died in 1937 most of her contemporaries had long gone, and the issues had changed irrevocably. The world had been at war and was gearing up to go to war again. There was nobody to write her obituary. Whereas if she had died in 1912 or 1917, the reputation she created with her early public life and then cemented with the Labour Commission and Prison Committee would have merited some notice in the press. That in turn might have captured the attention of the second-wave chroniclers of the first wave of the women's suffrage movement. But those scholars, in the 1970s and 80s, were researching in libraries and archives where the records put them at the mercy of Orme's own contemporaries, women and men who had never identified her as an independent single professional woman making her mark in public life. How could they? She blew through their lives like 'a comet or the north wind' and whether they admired her or not, they did not see her for what she was. Now that I am in a position to search for her name at a granular level in the press of the day, her substantial, though transient, contemporary reputation becomes apparent.

6. Journalism and Authorship

When I first set out to write about Orme's public life, I intended to include her journalism and other published writing along with the assignments, appointments and political commitments I discussed in Chapter 5. Rather to my surprise, the resulting chapter was too long and unwieldy. In any case, the notoriety that comes from journalism and authorship is different from the reputation that comes from political action and government service. As it turns out, Eliza Orme's journalism and authorship deserve a chapter of their own (and a bibliography as an appendix to this book). But like her practice of law and involvement in politics, they do not fit the standard and conventional categories.

It is well known, though not often remarked upon, that Victorians who are remembered for their writing generally concentrated on one genre or subject and they generally wrote pretty steadily, though not necessarily as their primary occupation. This holds especially when the material was journalism or essays rather than creative writing. Walter Bagehot wrote like that about politics, Harriet Martineau about economics, Frances Power Cobbe about philosophy; and each developed a reputation for discoursing on their specialty. Eliza Orme, however, did not have the luxury of journalistic specialization, and is consequently not remembered for her writing. Nevertheless, she had articles, essays, and books published on a wide variety of subjects, writing that appeared—sometimes signed and sometimes anonymously—when she had something to say and the opportunity to say it. If, back in 1984 when I first started my inquiries, printed reference works like the *British Library Catalogue* or *Reader's Guide to Periodical Literature* had not included citations to her publications, I would probably have given up right there. It was curiosity about the extraordinary range of her interests as revealed in print that kept me going.

©2024 Leslie Howsam, CC BY-NC 4.0   https://doi.org/10.11647/OBP.0392.06

For me, thinking about Eliza Orme's editorship of one weekly newspaper and her leading articles for another, her occasional articles in the mainstream press, and her authorship of government reports and other publications is an aspect of my studies of the history of the book and periodical press in Victorian Britain. Since the mid-1980s, historians and literary scholars have demonstrated that the mid-to-late nineteenth century was a time when authorship as a profession, publishing and printing as businesses, and reading as the pursuit of knowledge and pleasure, all burgeoned and flourished. Taken together, our growing knowledge of all those processes, as they connect and intersect, has become the study of Victorian book history. In nineteenth-century Britain, for the first time in history, some great novelists and essayists were able to make a career out of writing. At the same time, thousands of other writers submitted millions of words to the publishers of newspapers, periodicals, and books, sometimes signing their work and sometimes anonymous. Many of them could support themselves by their pens, while others struggled. (Orme's acquaintance George Gissing wrote about that phenomenon in *New Grub Street*.) The writers were supported and facilitated in turn by a handful of innovative publishers who worked to nurture those authors, and to turn a healthy profit for their own businesses and those of printers, binders, booksellers and others. The beneficiaries of all this were Victorian readers, for whom print was a great deal cheaper and more accessible than it had been for their ancestors. Barmaids, textile workers, even metal workers at the forge, as well as artists and lawyers and intellectuals and politicians—people of all classes—were eager readers. Cynics will note that the press in those days had no competition from the broadcast media, even from the cinema, let alone the internet, but the fact remains that every generation has its own 'new media'. It goes without saying that from childhood Eliza Orme was a reader of books, newspapers, and journals, of poetry and prose, of everything from fiction to law reports. Like many intelligent and ambitious young readers, she may have harboured the ambition to express herself in print when the opportunity arose. And, knowing how well-connected she and her family always were, the fact that she was acquainted with a publisher in Henry Lawrence, as well as with an editor or two, will not come as a surprise.

Contributions to *The Examiner, Englishwoman's Review* and *Longman's* (and an Index)

As far as I know Orme's first published venture came at the age of 25, when she wrote a brief signed article in *The Examiner* about 'University Degrees for Women' (July 1874). Her own studies at University College were well underway, even beginning to generate prizes and recognition, and she had recently consulted with Helen Taylor about her professional prospects. Furthermore, the subject of degrees was under discussion in the universities and in parliament. Orme's very temperate and reasoned column triggered a response in the *Saturday Review* three months later that ridiculed the very notion of women preparing to serve as doctors, lawyers, or clergy. She hit back with two more *Examiner* pieces, first returning to the subject under the original title, and then a fresh article. This time signed with her initials, it is entitled 'Sound-Minded Women'. She begins with a rather laboured comparison of clichéd ideas as they appear in art criticism and in political discourse. 'Old associations will go a very long way in making things which are mediocre in themselves the means of enjoyment'. This sets her up for her comments on the lack of originality in the anonymous *Saturday Review* writer's remarks about women and university degrees; I quoted from the article in Chapter 1.

It is not clear to me whether Orme was acquainted with the editor or the proprietor of *The Examiner*. It is possible. In any case, the next year, the same newspaper filled up a column with an unremarkable poem, 'Song' signed E.O. Those initials would not be enough to attribute the poem to Orme, but virtually the same poem appeared fifteen years later as 'Parted' in July 1890 in her own *Women's Gazette*, and that coincidence seems to me to clinch the matter. Artistically, it is not much of a poem, but it does remind me that the formidable debater and political strategist also wanted to make her emotional responses public, and she did not mind signing her verse with initials that would be identifiable to anyone who knew her.

In 1883 she wrote an obituary of the physician Matilda Chaplin Ayrton, one of the seven women who had struggled to open medical training at the University of Edinburgh. Orme and Ayrton were much of an age and must have been personally acquainted, through the Somerville Club if nowhere else. Orme remembered 'with a regret, amounting almost to bitterness, how much energy ... was in her case frittered away in fighting against the barriers set up in bigotry and self-interest'. Eliza's praise for Matilda's 'many-sidedness' might be applied to herself, too: 'She was able to study science minutely and accurately without becoming too selfish to be a politician, or too dry to be a sociable companion'. This article appeared in the *Englishwoman's Review*, as did one on Jeanette Wilkinson in September 1886. Wilkinson was among 'the small band of women who are earnest liberal politicians at this time'.

Eliza's next major signed article appeared in *Longman's Magazine*, in December 1886. Again she was hitting back, this time at a medical doctor. Benjamin Ward Richardson had written an essay on 'Women's Work in Creation' for the October issue that year, arguing that women must decide whether to become a rival or a helpmeet to men. This, in his view, required choosing between being unfeminine, grotesque, and unhealthy (even 'becoming a third sex'), or revelling in beauty, womanliness, attractive clothes and good health. At the time, Orme was profitably established in her Southampton Buildings chambers, doing patent agency and other legal work, and still a student at University College undertaking a series of competitive examinations. Women's work was perhaps becoming her signature issue, although there might also have been some personal and emotional impetus for writing the piece. She first called upon history and political economy to remind Richardson's readers that working-class women had always worked. Turning to women's intellectual labour, which was manifesting itself in new ways in their time, she focused on three issues. The first was dress, which Richardson thought was going to have to change drastically. But 'why', Orme asked, 'should it be more necessary for women to discard petticoats than for barristers to discard wigs? Petticoats are a slight incumbrance if the wearer desires to walk quickly, and are troublesome if she is out of doors in wet weather. Wigs are extremely irksome, and even unhealthy, when worn in a heated court of justice, and during the performance of highly intellectual work. If our judges and counsel are to be forgiven the little weakness of preferring fashion to comfort, the same leniency may be extended to self-supporting women of the educated classes'. Having thoroughly skewered the judges in her own field of expertise, she went on to compare the dark, tight, stiff-with-starch clothing of medical doctors like Richardson with 'the pleasant summer costume of what is called the advanced woman'.

Her second point noted Richardson's concerns about female beauty, but instead of seeing a trend to ugliness, she looked for evidence of contentment, noting 'an exchange from an expression of unsatisfied wishes in the face of an untutored girl to that of happy complacency in that of one now well taught what she has a taste for'. As for the third and perhaps most serious concern of the medical man—that overwork in cramming for examinations might impair women for conceiving and bearing children—she briskly undermined it. Women working as teachers, nurses, or in business need good health as much as mothers; and men need good health as much as women. Rather than require girls to choose between marriage and a career, 'If they are blessed with a good constitution, they may earn an honest livelihood either as the heads of their husbands' households or as independent workers'. She closed by suggesting that medical men like Richardson were unsuited by their training and professional experience to address social or political problems: 'They regard all human beings as passive patients, who are to have their failings examined, diagnosed, and prescribed for. They forget that unruly patients will refuse the prescription'. Eliza Orme's rhetoric in this article was practical as always, liberal in the small-l sense of the word, and characteristically witty.

While her journalism for *The Examiner* and *Longman's* was going on, Orme pursued another writerly project, although this time it was a work of legal scholarship, not of confrontational prose. Back when she entered the chambers of Savill Vaizey in 1873, she told Helen Taylor that she was 'helping him with his book on marriage settlements'. In 1887 that work finally appeared in two volumes: *A Treatise on the Law of Settlements of Property, Made Upon Marriage and Other Occasions*. It included Vaizey's acknowledgement of the invaluable assistance of 'my really, if not conventionally, learned friend', Eliza Orme, not least with the sixty-nine-page index. I note that Vaizey could not quite bring himself to use the common phrase 'my learned friend', but rather had to draw attention to the unconventionality of her being both learned in the law and female at the same time.

Leaders for the *Weekly Dispatch*

All the writing and indexing work I have described so far was signed or acknowledged. But there is evidence that Orme, writing anonymously, was one of the very few women working in the 'influential and highly-paid branch of newspaper work' known as leader-writing. A leader was a brief unsigned editorial opinion piece, composed in the 'voice' of the newspaper as a whole (in this case the *Weekly Dispatch*) on the news of the day. I have looked at the newspaper online, but because the leaders were anonymous and authoritative, I cannot tell whether she wrote the weekly commentaries on the minutiae of Liberal and Home Rule politics, the 'Women's Chit Chat' columns (themselves written from quite a serious viewpoint), or something else. Nor have I been able to ascertain exactly when this was going on, but it seems to have been in the late 1880s and early 1890s, the time of her life when she was busiest with her quasi-legal practice, with the politics of women's Liberalism, and perhaps even with the Royal Commission, because that was the time when the editor was one of her mentors. The *Weekly Dispatch* was a long-established Sunday paper with a radical bent, although by the 1880s it was cultivating a more sedate, middle-class readership and by the 1890s was reaching about 180,000 readers each week (according to *the Dictionary of Nineteenth-Century Journalism*). It had a number of editors in those years; one of them was W.A. Hunter, whose term of service was about 1887 to 1892. It seems to me that offering Eliza Orme a lucrative and influential platform for the expression of her strong opinions about Home Rule, women's rights, and other contemporary issues would not have been the first (or the last) thing that William Hunter, barrister and M.P., might have done to help his former student.

Because these leaders were anonymous, and no record appears to have survived conveniently attributing particular pieces to specific authors, I have not been able to confirm or expand on this information, which comes from an offhand remark in an 1891 *Monthly Packet* article on women in journalism by Fanny L. Green. As Green observed:

> Leader-writing is one of the most influential and highly-paid branches of newspaper work, but up to the present women have had but very small share in it. Probably there are very few of their number who possess the thorough training in history, philosophy, economics and politics, the mature judgment, and the power of clear, concise and forcible expression

that made Harriet Martineau's work in this direction so valuable and successful. ... Miss Power Cobbe has written leaders for the *Echo*, and Miss Orme has performed the same service for the *Weekly Dispatch*. Leader writing however, from the nature of things, cannot be entrusted to any one whose opinion does not carry weight with it. The leader writer is in no sense a tyro in letters.

Orme was no tyro (that is, novice) when it came to law and politics, and she had been an occasional contributor to the press for some years before her leader-writing for the *Weekly Dispatch*. But what is remarkable about this particular activity among her many professional and voluntary gigs is that Orme's leader-writing does not appear anywhere else in the evidence I have found about her legal and political work, or in her letters to Samuel Alexander. Of course it may not be true, although Green sounds like she knows what she is talking about and she was right about Martineau and Cobbe. If it is true, it merits further research, and will eventually have to be integrated into the narrative of Eliza Orme's life. For now, it can stand as an example of the many activities that left no trace—or in this case only a bare trace—in a long, full, and productive public life.

The *Women's Gazette* and the Royal Commission

Orme became editor of the *Women's Gazette and Weekly News* in 1889. Here, perhaps alongside her *Weekly Dispatch* leaders, she wrote regular editorials on the issues of the day. As with the other newspaper, I cannot attribute any of these anonymous 'leaders' to her authorship with confidence, but certainly many of them bear the unmistakable tang of her voice. Commenting on someone else's article about journalism as a profession for women, in November 1889, the leading article remarked:

> The mischief in many worthy women aspirants is that they are imperfectly equipped for the task. Every woman who can write a letter thinks she can write a paragraph, if not an article, but ten to one her grammar is unsound and her facts incomplete. Journalism needs as full a technical training as any other business or profession. When women realize that, they will find that a new world is open to them.

Somewhere along the line, Eliza Orme had acquired the necessary technical training. Other *Women's Gazette* leaders discussed Irish politics, or dress reform, or tried to educate other Liberal women not only about how to organize their peers, but about how not to antagonize the (male) party leadership.

Orme's next major writerly effort consisted of the several reports of the Royal Commission on Labour, coming out over a few months in 1892–93. She was sole author of the reports on barmaids and on the metal industries of the Black Country, collaborated with her colleagues on several of the others, and acted as supervising editor on the junior women's reports.

Because of the work of the Royal Commission, Eliza had to decline a prestigious invitation that came with the opportunity for international travel. She was invited to attend a Congress on Jurisprudence and Law Reform in Chicago. Having just finished traipsing all over England, Ireland, Wales and Scotland to interview barmaids and iron workers, however, and now engaged in writing and editing the reports, not to mention the invitation coming late, all she could spare the time for was to send a report on 'The Legal Status of Women in England'. Published in the *Albany Law Journal* on the 19th of August, 1893, the paper addressed the question of women serving as lawyers. She explained the technicalities of barristers and solicitors and how the profession itself and the institution of Parliament, respectively, acted as impenetrable barriers. Without identifying herself as one of the individuals in question, she added:

> Two women have been for some years practicing conveyance but without legal qualifications. They have drawn up wills and simple agreements, which under the English law may be prepared by persons not qualified as barristers or solicitors. Other conveyancing, such as drafting deeds, they have done for qualified practitioners, who have used the work in accordance with the maxim '*qui facit per alium, facit per se*'.

This legal term translates as 'The acts of an agent are the acts of a principle', while the legal convention permitted the in-demand barrister to be in two places at once, his own chambers and also Orme's.

Late in 1893, after the Royal Commission reports were published, circulated, and publicized, Eliza Orme returned to those chambers, now in Henrietta Street. Her political work resumed, but now with the new Women's National Liberal Association, not its rival Women's Liberal Federation. (If she did any writing for the WNLA 'Quarterly Leaflets', I have not yet been able to track it down.) The scandals of 1892 were now in the past, and the *Women's Gazette* had ceased publication. In the summer of 1894 came the opportunity of the committee on prison conditions, and later that year her meeting with George Gissing. Through the mid-nineties, the name of 'Miss Orme' appeared frequently in the national and local press—as a lecturer, or in reference to her reports on women's work in industry, or her leadership at a political meeting. There were also two major publications in 1897, on wildly diverging topics.

A Trial in India, a Literary Labour of Love, and More

Lawrence and Bullen, the company co-owned by Reina's brother Henry (and where Eliza Brabrook may have worked as a subeditor), published in 1897 a book on the subject of jurisprudence in India: *The Trial of Shama Charan Pal: An Illustration of Village Life in Bengal. With an Introduction by Miss Orme, LL.B.* It is the transcript of a courtroom trial, highlighting the skills of Manomohan Ghose as counsel for the defence. Orme framed her six-page introductory essay as being 'invaluable to those who consider it a duty to know something of the way in which the millions of our fellow-subjects in India are being governed'. The subject of law reform for Britain's colonial possessions in South Asia was then in turmoil. In addition, she noted, a recent novel was presenting 'biased and sensational pictures', as were the 'inaccurate and unverified accounts of Anglo-Indians returned to this country after years of official drill'. In her view, the report of a trial was 'obviously' the best way to get at the truth. It does not strike me as all that obvious, but what I do notice is that nine years earlier, a similar book had appeared from a different publisher. This time the introduction had been by Orme's law professor, mentor and (perhaps) editor/employer, William Hunter. It was *The Trial of Muluk Chand for the Murder of his Own Child: A Romance of Criminal Administration in Bengal. With an Introduction by W. A. Hunter* (1888, T. Fisher Unwin). The two books have been taken seriously, most notably in a scholarly article on the legal structures of colonial India by Vinay Lal. For my purposes, though, the question is not about the courts of Bengal, but rather about how Eliza Orme came to turn away from writing about issues with respect to women and work (not to mention re-establishing a precarious legal practice) to address a wholly new subject. Did the opportunity come from the publisher Henry Lawrence, the professor William Hunter, or from the lawyer Manomohan Ghose?

Ghose (1844–1896) was the first practicing barrister who was indigenous to the Indian subcontinent. He studied law in London and was called to the English bar in 1866, then returned to India to practice criminal law. He was known for being a proponent of women's higher education. As I speculated in Chapter 4, it is more likely that he and Orme met later. One documented encounter occurred when he returned to England in 1896 and she was in the audience while he debated the necessity of an independent judiciary in India. But Ghose had studied with Hunter, so the connection could have come from the professor, or from the publisher who wanted to build on the success of Hunter's book and knew that Eliza Orme had the brains and political savvy to address a question in a field unknown to her. I simply do not know. When I first learned about the book, I had exciting fantasies that Eliza Orme had travelled to India, perhaps had a whole life there quite separate from her existence in England. I do not think that anymore. It is much more likely that Ghose did the travelling, from the colonial outpost to the legal metropole. But I do think it possible that he and Eliza were friends as well as colleagues. He died the same year her book was published, and that factor may or may not have been significant.

Orme's second 1897 publication, an article in the mainstream journal *Nineteenth Century*, returned to a familiar subject. She defended the interests of unmarried women seeking professional careers. Once again, this was a response to something that annoyed her. A few months earlier, Frances H. Low had written in the same periodical about 'How Poor Ladies Live'. Orme had no dispute with Low about the sufferings of unmarried women who lacked adequate incomes, but she disagreed strongly about how their situation came about and how it might be cured. Low thought that the fathers of such women should continue to bear responsibility for their support. Orme estimated that it would take £1000 to provide for such a daughter in that way. 'But for less than a third of that sum a girl can be trained in a ladies' college for a useful breadwinning employment'. Nor must 'the Girton girl' be a teacher: 'At this moment highly educated women, bred in gentle homes, and retaining the affection and approval of their relatives, are working as milliners, dressmakers, clerks, bookkeepers, auditors, overseers in work-rooms, housekeepers, nurses, and in various other capacities in which, fifty years ago, they could not have employed themselves without loss of social status'. She also cogently pointed out that 'earners of money are spenders of money'. A professional woman, perforce, purchased the labour of milliners and dressmakers, servants, and a housekeeper. She might also help a younger sister or niece to get a start in life. Unlike Low, Orme understood that many women were 'improvident' about preparing themselves for independence because they expected to be married. To her, the remedy was obvious: 'The increased employment of women encouraged by college training, and by the taking up of paid work by ladies in a good position, tends to make the life of an unmarried woman so interesting that she will be less likely to regard marriage as the only goal'.

The year 1898 brought another article, and another book. 'Our Female Criminals' was published in another prestigious periodical, the *Fortnightly Review*. This time Eliza Orme was not responding to someone else, but taking advantage of her own experience and expertise to present her views to a much wider public than had access to the official report. And as she mentioned, 'the most important and far-reaching [of the recommendations] had been quietly ignored'. This was a chance to give them a fresh airing, and perhaps to put them before the eyes of a different set of decision-makers.

The book, however, was apparently a labour of love, or of homage. During the early years of the Women's Liberal Federation, Orme had worked closely with its founder, Sophia Fry. The two women were on the same side in the disputes over women's suffrage as Liberal Party policy, in strong opposition to the Countess of Carlisle. Lady Fry died in March 1897, and in May Orme wrote a brief account of her life for the *British Weekly*. A year later the book-length memoir appeared, published by Hodder and Stoughton. The introduction states that 'this slight sketch ... has been undertaken at the request of some of those who worked under her guidance in one or more of the public objects she had at heart'. The *Times* review commended 'the reticence and simplicity of Miss Orme's method' and observed that she had created an 'engaging but not too intimate picture'. When Liberal ladies gathered for their meetings, the advice was that 'a book such as Miss Orme's *Life of Lady Fry* might be read while the members knitted'.

I must admit I have never been able to get very excited about this particular work of Eliza Orme's. Like *The Trial of Shama Charan Pal*, it does not fit with her other publications. However, this one does not fit with her ideas either, apart from supporting the broad project of involving women in the work of Liberal politics. Perhaps she held her nose, as they say, believing the project required a tone that undermined her usual one of independence and self-reliance. It is pious, saccharine, and often seems to contradict the very things in which she ardently believed. ('Without denying the enormous strides made during the last fifty years in the education of girls, it may well be asked whether too great a sacrifice has not been made in giving up almost entirely the influences of home'.) Fry was the opposite of Orme's type of woman: married to a wealthy man; engaged in good causes. Her demeanour was domestic and reclusive, even while she was hard at work organizing other women in support of her male cronies in the Liberal Party. According to Orme's book, Fry's project had begun with Gladstone's Midlothian campaign and subsequent election in 1880 when many women (and men) came to understand that 'philanthropy and politics are inseparable'. In that election, Sophia's husband Theodore Fry was a successful candidate for Parliament. Six years later she founded the Women's Liberal Federation as an auxiliary to the party, to organize the labours of Liberal women. Whatever her personal diffidence, Sophia Fry was obviously a formidable organizer, and Eliza Orme (again, obviously) respected that. Beyond that, I simply do not know enough to hazard a guess as to why she wrote that particular book.

I suppose it is not quite impossible that Eliza had modified her views by the late 1890s, perhaps chastened by the experiences of the Royal Commission on Labour and the Committee on Prisons. No doubt they both involved numerous frustrations and humiliations. Not much had changed since the mid-1860s when Eliza had first written about 'sound-minded women' and the virtues of a university education and an independent career. Maybe she was burnt out. I do not really think so: her interview with the *Law Journal* was still to come on 12 December 1903, when she stoutly said 'perhaps I ought to have been more persistent' in the matter of trying to force her way into the Law Society and the ranks of solicitors. And an invitation to write the book—in the way that it had to be written—from Lady Fry's family and their mutual friends would have been difficult to refuse.

National Biography

Orme's next (and, as far as I know, last) appearance in print also took the form of biography. She wrote accounts of three lives for the 1901 supplementary volume of the *Dictionary of National Biography*. All of these men had died in 1898; the *DNB* editors had presumably commissioned Miss Orme for the task, having deemed them worthy of being memorialized. The men in question were William Alexander Hunter (1844–1898, lawyer), Samuel Plimsoll (1824–1898, 'the Sailors' Friend'), and Thomas Bayley Potter (1817–1898, politician). She seems only to have known Hunter personally, and indeed her sources for that essay were limited to 'private information', whereas such information was supplemented in Plimsoll's case by a couple of books and in Potter's by Hansard and 'personal knowledge'. Although she speaks formally, with a rigid correctness about all these men, as was the standard of the *DNB* and the custom of the period, her warmth for Hunter is discernible. When she wrote 'In 1875 ... he admitted women to his class in Roman law, and extended to them the same privilege when he afterwards became professor of jurisprudence' she must have remembered venturing into those masculine spaces herself and recalled Hunter's kindness to her, to Mary Ellen Richardson and Reina Lawrence, perhaps even to her sister Beatrice. She also mentions 'his intimate acquaintance with natives from India who had passed through his hands as law students', thinking again of Manomohan Ghose. Her other two subjects were perhaps better known than Hunter: Plimsoll's name is memorialized in the 'plimsoll line' painted on ships to ensure their safety at sea when carrying heavy loads, while Potter was a prominent MP and founder of a political society called the Cobden Club. Finally, all these three men had one more thing in common: they were ardent, active, Liberals in the same 'radical' tradition as Eliza Orme. And unlike most women contributors to the *DNB* she wrote not about other women, but about men.

I want to stress that most of the publications I have discussed here, and listed in the appendix, are signed with Eliza Orme's name. The exceptions are two or three pieces in *The Examiner* signed with her initials, some letters to the editor in the *Women's Gazette* where she wanted, presumably, to veil her own editorial identity, and the unknown number of leaders in the *Weekly Dispatch*. But I cannot list or discuss whatever articles or essays she may have written that I cannot find because they are unsigned. It is certainly possible that she wrote anonymously for one or more periodicals. Anonymity was the editorial policy of several journals and reviews, although that was changing by the late nineteenth century. And it is worth remembering, too, that her 'authorship' of complex legal documents under the names of male barristers was also, perforce, anonymous, however well-remunerated.

What did she *not* write about? Almost entirely absent from this account of Eliza Orme's contributions to written culture is anything about the law as a profession, still less about the experience of navigating a path to success at its quasi-professional fringes. She did, however, write about how the laws of marriage, of labour, and of property affected women in general, and much of her journalism is infused with the knowledge and assumptions that legal study had supplied. Also absent is any direct comment on her personal life, even when she wrote about someone she knew well (as with Sophia Fry and William Hunter) or about her own experience (as with prison policy or her writings on women's work and independence). Throughout her career as a minor public figure and an occasional journalist, she seems to have been careful to avoid the direct gaze of the reading public on her own life, her own mind and body. The more I have come to learn about her life, her interests, her values, her passions, the better I can understand the motives behind her published writing. But she remains elusive: who was Eliza Orme, and whose was she? What happened to her after that public gaze on her person and experience was removed?

7. Last Years

The following account of the last twenty years of Eliza Orme's life is sketchy, shaped by a handful of documents. Some of these are the kind of incontrovertible evidence produced by the state or preserved through the accident of a correspondent's eminence, while others are the more ephemeral scraps that have to be pieced together and supplemented by disciplined speculation. In the first category, we have her last letter to Samuel Alexander written in 1916 when she was sixty-seven; we also have the census record of her residence in a care facility in 1921 when she was seventy-two; and we have certification of her death, with a list of three causes, in 1937 when she was eighty-eight. Whereas the second category offers little more than a tangle of fragments, hints, absences, inferences and guesses.

Eliza's January 1916 letter to Sam Alexander is beautiful, warm, nostalgic and affectionate. The occasion was his fifty-seventh birthday; he had written to her when she turned sixty-seven a few weeks earlier. There was a terrible war going on, but she did not mention that. Instead, she remembered a new year's eve sixteen years earlier and recounted family news, some of it sad and some heartening. Her mind was clear and her voice strong, although she did report a recent illness. She wrote from home, from her own house in southwest London at number 118 Upper Tulse Hill, where she has just returned after staying with Reina Lawrence during a protracted recovery.

> Dearest Sam. I 'made a swear' as the children say to answer your letter today so as to wish you all the good old wishes for tomorrow. We were thinking of you last Friday night and recalling the night you spent here in 1899 when we, accompanied by your dog and our Rhoda walked down Tulse Hill and fancied we heard St Pauls Cathedral ringing in the new century. We heard all sorts of strange noises and the vague hum of the great city.

©2024 Leslie Howsam, CC BY-NC 4.0   https://doi.org/10.11647/OBP.0392.07

As for the illness, she does not specify her diagnosis, although it had been severe enough that Eliza and Beatrice temporarily broke up housekeeping to stay with the Lawrences at their Belsize Avenue house for over two months. Although she was now apparently recovered and returned to her own home, she referred to an ongoing 'stupid woolly condition' and observed that 'To hear of a friend's work is like a refreshing breeze when one is locked up in a sick room and it was good of you to let me have such a pleasant tonic'. She reported that:

> Beatrice and I led a lazy and luxurious life for ten weeks—or rather I did for Beatrice interrupted her rest cure to stay with Mrs Bastian until she was a little recovered from the shock of Dr Bastian's death. We knew he was very ill but the end was not expected and his keen interest in everything, especially in his own old work, made it very difficult to believe that the machine was going to stop.

She then shared news of the Masson family in Edinburgh, where Eliza's elder sister Rosaline had also just died, but her niece Flora was engaged in political writing and was herself interested in Samuel Alexander's intellectual work. All the Lawrence women were flourishing: the three unmarried sisters were doing philanthropic committee work, she told their mutual friend, exercising their excellent judgment and extensive experience in the aid of good causes.

This was the letter of a vigorous woman in her late sixties, speaking with pleasure about younger friends (Esther Lawrence was about fifty-four, and Caroline fifty-two, while Reina was fifty-five) who have come to maturity and the practice of successful careers, friends who are themselves beginning to slow down and retire into private life. Eliza herself was no longer a director of the Nineteenth Century Building Society, the property management organization she been part of for so long. Her name had not been in the news lately either, not since a few years earlier when activists were making an (unsuccessful) attempt to break down gender barriers to the practice of law and newspaper articles had referred to her labours as a conveyancer in the 1890s. But that was now far in the past. If she was being strictly accurate when she told the *Law Journal* in 1903 that she had practiced unofficially for twenty-five years, she might have stopped somewhere about 1900 (timing her start from the opening of the Chancery Lane chambers with Mary Ellen Richardson in 1875). She does not use the word, but let us say provisionally that she has retired. She continued to live for almost twenty years after the letter to Sam, no longer appearing in the press either with her own writings or in reports of public addresses or political work.

From my point of view as a researcher, Eliza's retirement—if that is what it was—means I have not been able to find out much more about her life after that 1916 letter. Not much, but something: five years later, when the census was recorded, she was living at Fenstanton, an institution in south London not far from the house at Tulse Hill. The place no longer exists; there is a school on the site. At the time it was described as 'a comfortable private asylum for ladies with mental and nervous disorders' that stood in twelve acres of wooded grounds and gardens. There were thirty beds. Twenty-one years later, she died at that same institution, perhaps merely of old age. To be specific, Madeline R. Lockwood (a woman doctor, not so rare by 1937) certified that the cause of death was in three parts: '(1a) senile gangrene of right foot; (1b) cardiovascular degeneration; (1c) senility'. Tissue death due either to infection or lack of blood supply (that is, gangrene) is unpleasant and painful, possibly associated with diabetes, but not in itself life-threatening. Almost everyone who gets to their late eighties has some sort of heart condition. But what did Dr Lockwood mean by 'senility?' Was that just a way of saying that her patient was very elderly, or had Eliza been suffering from dementia? And if the latter, how long had it been going on?

How do we bridge the gap between someone referring cheerfully to a 'stupid' and 'woolly' condition that kept her 'locked up in a sick room' in 1916 and a death-certificate notation of 'senility' in 1937? She did not sound like someone with Alzheimer's disease or any other form of dementia when she wrote to Sam. Perhaps those symptoms appeared within a few years and at some point before 1921 (when the census pinpointed her whereabouts) her sisters were not able to manage her at home. Only Beatrice was single and, in that sense, available, but she may have been unable to do what was needed. Or perhaps Eliza had a stroke that left her physically disabled; maybe she moved to Fenstanton of her own volition, convinced that they could care for whatever 'nervous disorder' she might have been diagnosed with. In that case, the brutal verdict on her death certificate might have emerged much later. I hope so, but I do not think I will ever know. Because the death certificate (like the record of her birth, and her will) was a legal document, I have had a copy of it since my first round of research, in the 1980s. It has always troubled me, and it still does. But now that I am older myself, now that a friend has come down with dementia, now that everyone in my generation is thinking about it—now I am ready to use it as a starting point for speculation, rather than as a grim end point to an extraordinary life.

Contemporaneities

One way to think about those last twenty-odd years might be to identify what was going on during the time of Eliza Orme's residence at Fenstanton. What happened to the people and causes that had captured her interest earlier? I find myself adopting the cultural historian's term, 'contemporaneity' (one scholar calls this concept 'the entangled now') to frame the questions. What was happening to the issues she was most passionate about? She was a Liberal, and Liberal governments beginning in 1906 made massive changes to Britain's social policy, many of which she had promoted. She was a pacifist, and there was brutal war in South Africa 1899–1902 followed by a horrific world war 1914–1918. Did she identify with the 'pro-Boers' who opposed the government's conduct in the first conflict, or with the 'conscientious objectors' who refused to fight in the second? She was a suffragist, and after the war legislation was passed to give women the right to vote in parliamentary elections. I would like to think she cast a ballot. She was a Home Ruler, and Ireland came to govern itself without reference to the British parliament. (Although that happened in a context of violence and uprising, and not as a matter of rationally decided legislation as imagined by people like Orme and her hero Gladstone.) She had aimed to practice law as a barrister or solicitor on the same terms as men, and in 1919 that right was granted to women by the Sex Disqualification (Removal) Act. It happened not long after she (probably) moved to Fenstanton. I hope she heard that news, but if she did, it must have been a bittersweet moment.

During those same decades, Eliza's housemate contemporaries were her oldest and youngest siblings: Charles Edward Orme, long retired from medical practice and fifteen years her senior, lived under Eliza's roof in Brixton until he died in 1912. At least that is what successive census records show; there is no further evidence of what he was up to. As for Beatrice Orme, when the household broke up a few years later she moved to Blanche Fox's home in Cornwall and lived there until she died, at ninety-two, in 1949.

Meanwhile, other members of the family and the families of their friends grew up, got older, had jobs and children; some of them died. Some of them embarked on successful careers, and in that case, records have survived. Eliza's Edinburgh niece Flora Masson became a nurse, working at that profession through the first world war (Florence Nightingale was her colleague and supporter). Flora and her sister Rosaline were active in the Scottish women's suffrage movement, and later Flora became a biographer and did some journalism. Their brother David Orme Masson emigrated to Australia and became professor of Chemistry at the University of Melbourne; Eliza kept in touch with this nephew and his wife. In her London sister Julia's family, the Bastians, there were three sons and two daughters: Charles Orme Bastian was an electrical engineer and inventor. (Did Aunt Eliza help out with patents?) James Bastian, a commercial traveller, also emigrated to Australia but later returned to England with his family. William Bastian was a staff surgeon in the Royal Navy. May Bastian (who followed her aunt Eliza to University College) married Edward Upton Strick a land agent. Sybil Bastian stayed single; she handled the sale of some family mementoes to the National Portrait Gallery in 1952. Among Eliza's Fox nephews (the sons of Blanche, living in Cornwall), Howard Orme Fox was an imperial civil servant and later a judge in Ceylon (now Sri Lanka); his brother Charles Masson Fox expanded his father's business as a timber merchant in Cornwall. Outside the Orme clan, Eliza's dear friend Samuel Alexander continued to practice as one of Britain's leading philosophers. Sam's brother Maurice taught music. Among the 'Belsize family', Reina Lawrence's sister Esther became head of Froebel College and hence a pioneer of early childhood education. Henry Walton Lawrence continued as a publisher until 1900 and later worked for the Medici Society. The eldest Lawrence sibling, Laurie, was an ear, nose, and throat surgeon and, in his private life, an aficionado of stamps and coins. His brother Arthur Moss Lawrence was a barrister and a businessman, keeping up the family's connection with the source of its American playing-card fortune. Another Lawrence sibling, Gerald, was an actor on the stage and in silent films. Even if Eliza Orme came to be forgotten by her allies (and adversaries) in the women's suffrage movement, she had many people to remember her who were alive and flourishing through her years of retirement.

Other suffrage-movement contemporaries, both allies and adversaries, probably lost track of Eliza Orme as they all got older. Many of those women had gone through the traumatic weeks of the dissolution of the Women's Liberal Federation in 1892, when Miss Orme was perceived as either 'a comet or the north wind' (to recall the language of the *British Weekly* profile). Her comet appeared in the political realm and briefly lit up the sky with the exhilarating possibility of introducing articulate and practical women into the spaces of politics, and eventually of government, as the equals of men. The comet fell to earth when Lady Carlisle manoeuvred Miss Orme out of the majority leadership of the WLF and into a position where the necessity of adhering to principle meant exclusion from power and influence, at least within the party. Her north wind had briefly been a blast of common sense blown through an otherwise timid political cohort, but it was too cold, austere, and practical to attract a lot of support. According to the biography *Radical Countess*, Lady Carlisle eventually came to regret her campaign to make women's suffrage a plank in the Liberal platform. But that reversal was of no use to Eliza Orme or to the other women whose lives, decades later, were still affected by that quixotic crusade.

Of course, it is possible that Eliza knew nothing of any of these contemporaneities—that her move to Fenstanton about 1917 was caused by the dementia that appeared on her death certificate twenty years later. Evidence to the contrary might have been lost, or perhaps exists in a family archive in Australia, or among the descendants of her Edinburgh, London, and Cornwall families. I would like very much to know, but it does not really matter. She disappears from the public record as an active participant around 1903, when she was in her mid-fifties. Since women at that point mostly did not work as professionals and by definition could not retire from professional practice, it would be anachronistic to think of this disappearance as evidence of 'retirement'. Perhaps the invitations to public service gradually dried up, along with opportunities to do occasional journalism. Or perhaps they continued to arrive, but she declined the offers. Beatrice or Reina or someone else might have needed her undivided attention. The house on Tulse Hill might have required extensive repairs that she was unwilling to undertake. She and Beatrice might have been low on money. Or so comfortable that they no longer needed to work.

Retirement

All this raises a research question for historians: what did 'retirement' mean to unmarried professional, or semi-professional, women who came of age late in the nineteenth century? There were so few of them that their situations may have varied too much to make any generalizations. Or perhaps the investigation is just waiting to be undertaken. As it happens, we are only just beginning to realize what retirement means now, to women like me who came of age in the second-wave-feminist 1960s, created careers, reputations, and legacies for ourselves by the early twenty-first century, as lawyers, professors, politicians, civil servants, and leaders in all walks of life. Women have always worked, both in the labour market and in our own homes, but we have only recently begun to 'retire' in the sense of reaching a milestone birthday, terminating an employment contract, coming to the end of nine-to-five commitments and the beginning of voluntary engagements, and perhaps even starting to collect a pension. I was sixty-seven when I retired in that sense, from teaching and doing my share of academic administration, and left the university behind. Ten years later, I am still figuring out what retirement means. When Eliza was sixty-seven, she had probably been finished with her quasi-professional labours for a dozen or so years. But the comparison is meaningless, since she was never an employee, and mandatory, or even customary, retirement ages were still far in the future.

The circumstance that Eliza Orme died at such a great age (eighty-eight) after having started so very young (only nineteen) in the women's suffrage movement, is almost enough to explain why her name scarcely turns up in the memoirs and annals of her contemporaries. Even apart from her political differences in the 1890s with some who wanted to put the vote ahead of every other cause, she did not fit in demographically with that cadre of redoubtable women we call moderate suffragists and militant suffragettes. She was somewhat younger than the first group, and much older than the second. More importantly, she was single and self-supporting, while many of them were either married to sympathetic husbands, widowed with significant means, or the unmarried daughter-heirs of wealthy men who had died conveniently young. Her education in mathematics, political economy, and law enabled her to forge a career in law, politics, and public policy. Other educated women could work in one or two of those areas, and did: I cannot think of anyone else who managed all three, unless it was Reina Lawrence. But Lawrence chose to enter politics directly, in London County Council elections as soon as women were eligible. And her focus seems to have been on local issues.

What Eliza Orme aspired to may have been much more ambitious, if I am right that she aimed to sit among the first women members of the British Parliament. While waiting for that role to open up in a practical way, though, she created and seized opportunities when possibilities presented themselves. She wanted to be the person asked to serve on a royal commission (not merely to be a factory inspector), probably angled for the job, and got it. She advised about how both working-class and middle-class women should conduct their working lives (while conducting her own exceptional enterprise). She sought to guide the political education of other Liberal women so they could become the leaders of the next generation (while her contemporaries were caught up in the struggles of particular moments). Once those objectives and experiences were played out, however, neither her contemporaries nor her successors, and neither her allies nor her antagonists, seem to have recognized the distinctiveness of Eliza Orme's ambitions, and the singular way she thought about how to achieve them.

If these speculations are anywhere near correct, perhaps what 'retirement' meant to Eliza Orme was a recognition that the moment had passed, the moment for her to move fully into the mainstream of political life and use her training, experience, and capacities to the full. It would not be surprising if, by 1917 or perhaps earlier, she was disillusioned with her contemporaries. Even her allies among Liberal women did not understand or acknowledge her analysis of how the party auxiliary should function. As for the powerful men in her circle, even those who respected her talents were not prepared to accept her leadership as part of the mainstream, but only to see her manage the auxiliary. She must have been bitterly disappointed, too, with the lack of action emerging from her reports on working conditions and later on prisons, not to mention what had become of the Women's Liberal Federation. If policymakers and allies are not listening, and your personality calls for a quiet, clever campaign of persuasion (and if you are tired and not very well) it might seem eminently practical just to stop pushing, stop leading, and retire to private life.

8. Who Was Eliza Orme?

Eliza Orme was a remarkable woman whose life should be remembered, and not only because she achieved the status of first woman in England to earn a university degree in law. She became a property conveyancer and patent agent, a significant achievement that gets overlooked because she could not be a barrister or solicitor. She was a figure in the early days of the women's suffrage movement, but her leadership there was complicated by other people's meddling. She trained Liberal women in the skills of political organization and rhetoric, but that legacy, too, was compromised. She was a prolific writer, but one with eclectic interests that set her apart from journalists. Her private letters reveal an affectionate, loyal, sweet woman, but letters are difficult to interpret without a life to attach them to. Similarly, fragments derived from newspapers, or from the lives of others, demonstrate that her public life was extraordinary but evanescent, briefly in the spotlight and then anonymous again until someone remembered to call upon her. People interested in the same issues she cared about knew who she was, but may never have asked about her motivations. Or if they did, they did not leave a record of the conversation. In any case, in the nature of things, a lot of what she did remained private and unrecorded.

Stripping away all those 'buts' and archival absences, we are still left with the questions of who she was, and both why and how she should be remembered. My research has turned up some answers to the first question. She was striving, secure, and assertive. With trusted associates she could be witty and often sarcastic; with those she cared for, she was playful, sparkling, loveable; but out in the world her demeanour was reticent and dignified. She was a competent professional who was not recognized by the accrediting bodies of her profession. She was always precariously employed, but in extraordinary roles. Among her political colleagues she was known to be loyal, organized, and influential, a

 https://doi.org/10.11647/OBP.0392.08

strategist with smart ideas and a plan for implementation. In her own mind, she was practical and logical. I think the key to all this is that she was both hugely ambitious and deeply disappointed, but I have no way to ask her how she would like to be remembered. A summing-up chapter, then, has to start with who she is to me.

Eliza and Me, since 2016

I am not the only person who has taken an interest in Eliza Orme. Mary Jane Mossman properly identified her as a forerunner of the first women lawyers. Gissing scholars labelled her as a competent associate who assisted their man in his hour of need. Researchers with an interest in barmaids and metal workers, in the prison system, in Indian jurisprudence, have come across her writings and cited them with as much context as was available. Some who want to reclaim the queer identity for Londoners of her period have suggested that she belongs in that category. But I am the only one who has tried to study her on her own terms. During the years when my career took another direction, I never quite forgot about her and never quite accepted the prevailing judgment that she was not interesting enough to warrant significant research. I was disappointed that my 1989 *Atlantis* article did not seem to gain any traction among feminist historians of Britain. I told myself that her story didn't fit in with their intellectual debates (and I did not know then that Mossman was reading it). When, in about 1992, the editors of the *Dictionary of National Biography* announced that they were going to produce the 'Missing Persons' volume, gathering in the people whose lives had not been deemed important enough by generations of their editorial predecessors, I diffidently offered her as a subject and was accepted. That enterprise produced results: my first correspondence with the Gissing scholar Pierre Coustillas came as a result of it. Identifying her as a 'missing person' was deeply satisfying, and on the strength of it I wrote to an American publisher of trade biographies in 1994, proposing one of Eliza Orme. They politely replied that her life was probably not sufficiently extraordinary to capture the interest of general readers.

The next thing that happened was much later, after I had retired in 2014. This was the renewed interest in Orme that came about as women lawyers and legal scholars began to anticipate the 2019 centennial of legislation permitting women to practice law in Britain. It was gratifying to be asked to speak at a 2016 symposium on the First Women Lawyers in Great Britain and the Empire, and later to write a blog post about her for 'The First 100 Years' project celebrating the anniversary. But at the same time it was troubling to realize how some of that community framed her as a 'precursor' or even as a 'failure'—as someone who did not manage to become a fully-fledged lawyer. (As if that would ever have been possible in the 1870s and 1880s; as if 1919 did not come along too late to matter, in career terms, for anyone born in 1848.) I recognized that their framing set Orme outside the conversation about the women lawyers who did manage that feat, so that her achieving the degree and the quasi-professional practice did not seem to count—or not quite. It was very helpful for me to identify that frustration, and realize that if Orme is worth remembering, it has to be for what she did do, not for what she did not. And perhaps for what she might have done. In retrospect, I think that feeling defensive of her reputation became an important part of my persistence. I wanted to write her story, and that meant trying to figure out what she herself thought about women and the practice of law while recognizing that was not necessarily the defining motive of a long and complex life.

Around the same time as the legal scholars started gearing up for a celebration, a new generation of feminist historians began asking questions about professional work in the decades at the turn of the twentieth century. Brilliantly, in a way the scholars who studied 'professionalization' in earlier years had never thought to do, Heidi Egginton and Zoë Thomas and others introduced the question of precarity. If there were barriers to women and other marginalized people working as highly skilled professionals, then their situation could fairly be characterized as precarious. The feminist historians of my own generation had never shown much interest in Orme, but it turned out that the ones who were young enough to have been our students found her appealing. And their conceptualization of precarity and professionalism was an eye-opener for me. The result was my chapter for Heidi's and Zoë's *Precarious Professionals* volume of 2021.

It was a deeply satisfying coincidence when my knowledge as a historian of books, periodicals, and publishing began to enhance my research on Eliza Orme, and vice versa. I have to admit that for a long time I did not take her editorship of the *Women's Gazette* seriously enough. This changed with the realization that the Women's Liberal Federation's own copy of the closing issues of the newspaper had not been irretrievably lost, and that I could get my hands on digital scans of each and every page. The result was my 2022 article in the journal *Victorian Periodicals Review*, published by the Research Society for Victorian Periodicals (RSVP). I have been part of the leadership of RSVP, as I have of the Society for the History of Authorship, Reading, and Publishing (SHARP). I would not understand Eliza Orme as author, as journalist, and as editor the way I do, if it were not for my 'day job' as a historian.

A centrally important aspect of my identity as a historian has been coming to understand the way that historical scholars think, what kind of questions we ask about the past, how we read the documentary evidence, and when it might be safe to speculate. I learned to think that way too, through my experience of doing a master's degree and then the coursework and comprehensive reading required for a doctorate, then being guided by historians through the writing of a dissertation, and later learning about collegiality and pedagogy by practicing my discipline in an academic appointment. Many, perhaps most, of my colleagues take thinking like a historian for granted, but for me that was impossible because I found myself engaged in an interdisciplinary pursuit. Literary scholars, librarians, and others are also studying the histories of books and of the periodical press, but they think like people trained in those disciplines. I have made this insight central to my scholarship: in books and articles and keynote addresses, I have urged repeatedly that 'book historians' who come from whatever background should be respectful of the boundaries between the various disciplinary approaches to our protean subject. The fact that interdisciplinarity is valuable does not mean that book history is itself a single discipline. Recognizing this essential aspect of disciplinarity and interdisciplinarity probably hit me so hard because so much of my graduate-school experience was shaped by a literary scholar who did not himself respect the boundaries. But now I realize that my peculiar experience of higher education made me who I am. The reason I mention it here is because I also realize that it was her professional education that made Eliza Orme who she was, even while it did not make her a lawyer.

I have learned, from friends who are legal academics and whose job it is to train the next generation of working lawyers, that the way lawyers are taught how to think is peculiar to their discipline and profession, perhaps even more than with historical or literary studies. It is not easily acquired; it is difficult for outsiders to understand; it is often hard for lawyers to explain or justify their ways of thinking to outsiders; nor are they required to do so. (Insert joke here about their high fees, but that is not the point I am trying to make.) The law is a complicated cultural construct. It is an agreed-upon arrangement for making society work under stress, whether the challenge comes from international affairs or federal-provincial relations or business contracts or personal security. Law students learn that while the objective of law is justice, the interpretation of law, both at the point of legislation and later in the courts, does not always bring about justice. They learn that law is inextricably connected with politics and history, because laws are made by elected officials, inside the constraints of particular governments operating at specific moments. That is the gist of what Eliza Orme learned from her professors and mentors, whether they spoke explicitly to her about those principles or not.

This insight has been crucial in my understanding of how she conceptualized the women's suffrage movement during the 1880s and 1890s. For a long time, that question was a source of anxiety to me: was she a feminist and suffragist, or was she not? She was, but there is a crucial caveat and it is not just that she was a feminist suffragist Liberal. It is that Orme thought like a lawyer, whereas her friends and colleagues (and her adversaries, too) thought like laywomen, like non-lawyers. Her allies in the Women's Liberal Federation understood politics pretty well, and that enabled them initially to work together, especially since their objective was explicitly not to press the Gladstonian Liberal Party to make women's suffrage a matter of party policy, but rather to bring about Home Rule for Ireland. Those allies still did not think within the framework of the law, but merely in terms of political organization and electoral strategy. Whereas Rosalind Howard the Countess of Carlisle, and people like her, were not concerned with working within the constraints of either politics or law, but rather with promoting justice. Theirs were two diametrically opposed ways of thinking about the same cause.

Eliza Orme was a feminist, passionately committed both to women's suffrage and to the provision of opportunities for women to take their places in the workforce at all social levels. Scholars of the first wave of feminism in Britain are still arguing about the relative value of moderate 'suffragist' policy and the militant 'suffragette' movement that flourished later. We understand a lot better now that the law and politics are gendered, that laws and policies are sexist (and racist, and inflected by assumptions about class superiority, physical ability, and all the other ways to marginalize people). That understanding, however, is the legacy of the second wave of feminism, which makes it difficult to comprehend the conflicts that divided members of the first wave. In the Women's Liberal Federation of the early 1890s, the Countess of Carlisle was right in her doggedness and clarion call for justice for women. But her timing and tactics were wrong. There were better places to make a stand than an auxiliary of Gladstone's embattled Liberal Party. Eliza Orme was right too, when she said that 'nothing would assist the cause like practical work done by women'. But it did not happen the way she anticipated; when the laws finally changed about women's suffrage (and women's admission to the legal professions), it was after a world war that had demonstrated women's practical competence. It is important for me to acknowledge that Lady Carlisle was right, but that is not really my point, either. My point is that Eliza's legal education— an experience she shared only with Reina Lawrence and a tiny handful of other women—set her irrevocably apart from her peers. It made her think, not only like a lawyer, but to some extent like men of her class and background. Her own characterization of this mode of thought was that she was 'hopelessly practical', but that robust depiction concealed her capacity to understand and influence a delicate political and personal situation.

Loyalty, Logic, and Strategy: The Case of Charles Dilke's Divorce Scandal

I have come to see Eliza Orme as a sophisticated, cosmopolitan person of wide experience and a habit of discretion, well aware that unconventional behaviour and relationships could flourish outside the bounds of respectability. This awareness was something else that set her apart from many middle-class women at a time when public opinion could be censorious. Probably she knew and kept many secrets that have remained private. One exception may be the case of Charles Dilke, where there is tentative evidence, in an 1886 letter to Samuel Alexander, that she was privy to the politician's situation. Dilke went to court in that year, accused by Donald Crawford of seducing his wife Virginia. Donald claimed that Virginia had confessed to the affair and Dilke, on the advice of lawyers and colleagues, refused to give evidence of his own innocence. (The situation was murky since Dilke was carrying on an extra-marital relationship, but it was with Virginia Crawford's mother, and Virginia herself was related by marriage to Dilke's brother.) When Dilke, again badly advised by his lawyers, tried to reopen the case he was attacked and humiliated, first in court and then in the press. Many people, including members of the Women's Liberal Federation, were shocked, titillated, and prepared to believe the worst, but Orme admired Charles Dilke as a politician and counted both him and Emilia Dilke as friends.

I say the evidence is tentative because no names are mentioned in the letter, but the dates match up and so do Orme's remarks about the details. Furthermore, Alexander received a letter five months later from Lady Dilke, referring to heavy misfortunes and 'foul lies' about her husband. Apparently Sam had sought Eliza's advice and suggested that Dilke might eventually retrieve his wounded reputation by good work in public life. In her reply, Eliza told Sam that she had been 'much concerned' in the case and encouraged her friend to take a generous view. She asked him:

> Should we any of us be trampled upon in this way if a maniac or a liar or an enemy brought a grave accusation against us and, acting under high professional advice, we blundered amongst the technicalities of law courts and failed to do exactly what public opinion demanded? If so then we are all walking on the edge of a precipice. If it is the person's previous character that settles it then I put the opinion of intimate friends of many years standing and the undeniable fact of happy family life against the gossip of comparative strangers and political enemies. One especially circumstantial story I chanced to have the means of testing and though it had been often repeated during the last election and sworn to by men and women pretending to be responsible for its truth, I find it to be absolutely false. The details are true but the person concerned was a

different man living in the same locality with a somewhat similar name and the same title. I take this as a test case and put the rest down as of about equal value.

Another thing I cannot understand is the way in which men having experience of the grave responsibility of public life can for a moment forget that this man said in a letter addressed to representative constituents 'I am entirely guiltless of the charges brought against me'. Such a deliberate statement made with the object of retaining the confidence of the electors would be false, be by far the most disabling act that he could possibly be guilty of. No one could trust him for public service if he put his name to a deliberate lie with the object of being elected. Either that statement was true or false. If you believe he spoke the truth—and he has always been known as a truthful man—you are bound to do your utmost in any way that happens to be possible to you to cheer his present time of trouble and prevent the permanent injury of his chances of public work. If you believe he told this deliberate and profitable lie how can you say that he may retrieve himself by good work? Can a man *retrieve* a leg lost by amputation if he is to be a professional runner? A deliberate lie told with the object of self interest is surely as irretrievable in the career of a public servant.

The conscientious sifting of evidence and the absolute refusal to be affected by rumours seems to me to be the tone we most need in these newspaper-interviewing days. General disbelief would discourage the abominable trade. And besides the general good in this case strong personal liking makes me think much all round the question. So forgive a lengthy screed. At any rate it needs no answer.

Whether or not this screed referred to the Dilke case, it would be of great interest to know the exact nature of Orme's 'concern', and in particular whether she was involved in initiating the proceedings of the acrimonious Crawford divorce case.

Nor was she prepared to abandon him in 1892 when Dilke sought re-election (and to re-establish his reputation and political career) in the Forest of Dean constituency, just because Lady Carlisle and others in the WLF were offended by the old rumours stirred up at that time. But the rumours persisted. Another woman law graduate, Cornelia Sorabji, wrote to a friend in 1898 that she did not want to be 'a kind of Miss Orme [known to] put in train ugly divorce proceedings'. It is impossible to know whose divorce this refers to. Not the Gissing breakup in 1897, which was only a separation, and if she was talking about the Crawford divorce, Orme's 'concern' has not shown up in the course of Kali Israel's extensive recent research on those proceedings. (Although if her intervention in the case was discreet, it would have been known only to someone like Sorabji who probably kept her eye on a fellow woman legal practitioner's activities.) Eliza was a loyal friend: even after his death she raised money for the Dilke Memorial Hospital. I can say all that with considerable confidence, but it is only because I can guess who Eliza was probably talking about when she advised Sam Alexander about how to handle his interactions with Emilia Dilke at the time of the original scandal.

Speculation: Eliza's Thwarted Ambition

In the course of writing this book, I have identified Eliza Orme as ambitious, but I can only speculate as to her ultimate aim in life. I have not a scintilla of direct evidence to demonstrate that she wanted to become one of the cohort of Britain's first women Members of Parliament. In the event, that was just as unthinkable an outcome as to be called to the bar. I find it quite reasonable to imagine an optimistic young person of the late 1860s planning a career based on the expectation that women's suffrage would become law in time for her to take advantage of its affordances. With votes for women, surely there would be opportunities for someone who positioned herself for them by taking a prestigious university degree and then serving her chosen party with loyalty and energy. Once that party was in power, the archaic rules that barred women from being called to the bar could change. Or something even better might emerge. She was a close friend of Charles Dilke who (until his scandal) was talked about as a future Liberal Prime Minister. She was well acquainted with John Stuart Mill and other powerful politicians. One way or another, I think the young Eliza crafted a strategy and acted upon it: academic work, journalism and political service to build a reputation, then take advantage of opportunity when it came. Events did not work out the way she might have expected, but then they seldom do.

Each element of her strategy (if that is what it was) produced results: her conveyancing, patent, and financial work; her editing, public speaking, and writing; her passionate interest in Ireland's land law; her being commissioned and appointed to policy work. With the Inns of Court, the Law Society, and the Liberal Party remaining obdurately unchanged, however, the separate elements never fused together into a single coherent career narrative. Because so much evidence is lost, not least the evidence of discrimination and roadblocks put directly in her way, it is certainly possible to speculate that she had some other ambition in mind. Still, this is the one that makes sense to me: political service not at the local level like other ambitious women of her generation, but in the Parliament of the United Kingdom.

I have come to regard Eliza Orme as a woman of presence in British society, someone that people knew and respected. At the same time, though, she did not fit the customary roles. Perhaps nobody was quite sure what to make of her. She was independent when most women were not. She was practical when many independent women were artists and visionaries. She was influential, often behind the scenes with men who held power, but she did not entangle herself in their projects. I almost see her as acting a bit like one of the 'grandes dames' of her time—the society hostesses who knew everyone and whose behind-the-scenes intervention could change the course of a parliamentary enquiry or a courtship. But only a bit, because unlike most of those ladies, Orme had neither husband nor sons in her orbit. That must have been disconcerting for the women and men who knew her. She exercised charm as well as intelligence, enjoying both work and leisure. In public she supported the causes she cared about, while she could still walk in private with friends across country on a fine day, all of them arrayed in comfortable ulsters and practical tam o'shanters.

Who was Eliza to Her Friends and Family?

Back in the 1980s, the only personal thing I knew about Eliza Orme was that she smoked a cigar after a private dinner party; now I know a lot more, even that she disliked Christmas cards and had a dog called Rhoda. But I still do not know whether at any stage in her long friendship with Reina Lawrence it became a sexual one. I do not know why she wrote more warmly to Samuel Alexander about Reina's 'Belsize family' than about her own brothers and sisters, or much of anything about the dynamics of her family of origin. (Nor do I know whether the 'other family at Buxton' she mentioned to Sam was a significant part of her life, or even who those people were.) Surely someone who wrote as affectionately as Eliza did to Sam must have had other people in her life who heard that same pleasant voice, who knew the passion of Eliza's personality—but they threw her letters in the fire after replying to them.

Eliza Orme's will throws light on some of these questions and fortunately that document has survived intact, right down to her handwriting. It was dated 20 August 1885, identifying her as being 'of 27 Southampton Buildings in the county of Middlesex, Spinster'. She was then thirty-six years old, still studying law but already practicing in those professional chambers near Chancery Lane. The witnesses were Elizabeth and Emma Hull, both 'of 2, The Orchard, Bedford Park' so presumably servants in the family home where Eliza still resided (although not for the purposes of this document). Both her parents were alive that summer, as were all Eliza's siblings except Helen (died 1857) and Campbell (whose 1883 death might have precipitated the decision to express her wishes). She had an elder brother who was a surgeon, one brother-in-law a medical researcher, another a professor, and a third in business, as well as the long list of nephews already noted. She also had a long-standing lawyer, S.N.P. Brewster. All of these obvious male candidates for executor she ignored, and instead appointed 'my dear friend Reina Emily Lawrence' for that task. Two people were to benefit from her estate: Beatrice would receive 'all my money and securities for money', and Reina 'all my real estate and all my residuary personal estate'. In the end, presumably, everything went to Beatrice, since the house had long been sold, but had Orme died younger, the already wealthy Reina Lawrence would have been an important beneficiary. Lawrence's status as executor and beneficiary, given the date of the will, is the solidest evidence we have of the seriousness of their relationship. Leaving her money to Beatrice makes sense, since the two youngest Ormes, and the only two to remain 'spinsters' had long since formed a bond. The probate record showed that the total value of the estate was £787.15s.8d (roughly £125,000 in the 2020s). While that is not very much money, it is not surprising given the many years between Orme's peak earnings and her demise. The death certificate gives her address as 37 Belsize Avenue, Hampstead. This was, or had been, the Lawrence family home and was presumably taken from the Fenstanton patient records. By this time, however, Reina had a house of her own in the country, near Kelveden in Essex.

If Eliza Orme was as cosmopolitan and discreet as we know she was, and at the same time people did not quite know what to make of an independent professional woman with political interests, where did her private self fit into the gender hierarchy of an inherently patriarchal society and culture? Specifically, did she identify herself, in any sense, as a woman who loved women? Can we call her 'queer'? I do think she probably loved Reina Lawrence and it is possible that they were open about their arrangements when with trusted friends. (Maybe that is why Sam was disinvited to the walking party in the Highlands of Scotland; and perhaps that is how one of Paul Delany's biographical sources got hold of the idea of a 'Boston marriage', and why a recent chapter by Kellie Holzer calls her a 'woman-identified woman'.) But I do not think we can call her queer as far as the public figure is concerned. Today's terminology would say that her public self-presentation was heteronormative. Beyond that, I suspect that she did not fit in with many men, beyond superficially. It may have been the same with most women: even those who shared her ends envisioned different means. But she did fit in with friends and family who took her seriously. Whatever she did behind closed doors, my analysis of her intentions and ambitions seems to preclude any wish to identify herself with other women in terms of sexuality. As 'Miss Orme' she stood out as a person with a female sobriquet, but she also fitted in, as a person of expertise with well-thought-out opinions and solid experience.

Apart from her relationship with Reina, there are questions to be asked about her position in the family, in particular during her retirement years in the house at Tulse Hill. It might seem odd that a single woman, the second youngest of six surviving siblings, would end up the head of the family, but then she was head and shoulders more able than any of them and probably impatient with dithering. Census returns reveal that Eliza Orme was head of a household that included a professional man who was much older than herself, her brother Charles Edward. However it seems pretty clear that she, not he, was the owner or leaseholder of the house in which the household resided, and the person who made the decisions. Her father's will left £5,446 to his three unmarried children, Charles, Eliza and Beatrice. Eliza was executor. Maybe that is why they all lived under the same roof. (There is a gap between Charles Orme's death in November 1893 and the move to Tulse

Hill; the timing is unclear but the move was some time before October 1895.) And if she was head of the household she shared with her siblings, might she also have been regarded as the head of the extended Orme family and keeper of the family record? One might expect one of the older, married, sisters to take on that role, but perhaps each of them was oriented to her husband's family. When Eliza's niece Sybil Bastian sold family treasures through Sotheby's in 1952, the record stated that ownership of one of them had passed from Mrs Charles Orme to 'Miss Orme 1917' to Sybil Bastian. I suspect that ambiguous note (to be found in the Rossetti Archive) means that Eliza received the treasures from her mother and then passed them on to her unmarried niece when she moved to Fenstanton, which would have been round about 1917. These objects included the drawing of Holman Hunt made by Dante Gabriel Rossetti (given by Hunt to his patron and friend the senior Eliza Orme and now in the National Portrait Gallery) and possibly the two medallions by Woolner, one of Tennyson, and the other of Helen Orme, the latter presented to her mother a few years after Helen's death.

Conjecture about these connections of family, friendship, and inheritance is supported by at least a thread of evidence. It is a lot more speculative when the record is lacking altogether. Take the case of Manomohan Ghose, the barrister from India whose book she edited. I do not think it too far-fetched to speculate that the two of them might have felt a kinship with each other, based upon the shared experience of being outsiders, eager and brilliant, but kept at arm's length by the legal establishment in London. They could even have been close friends, carrying on a correspondence as rich as Orme's with Samuel Alexander and producing a body of (hypothetical) evidence, since lost or destroyed.

Who Was Miss Orme to Lawyers (Then and Now)?

One of the biggest gaps in the evidence is about how Orme constructed her quasi-professional life. How did she manage the quotidian responsibilities of a conveyancer, a patent agent, a barristers' trusted assistant, and a mortgage broker? She gave Helen Taylor the impression that the work came easily to her and Mary Richardson, but they may have courted disapproval by marketing their services in Chancery Lane during those early years. The transition from Vaizey's office to their own chambers, on Phipson Beale's advice, might have been fraught with anxiety. While that move seems to have turned out well, I have no doubt that there were male barristers who declined to take advantage of what their 'miniature Girton' offered, assuming that women could not possibly do exacting legal work at that level. In addition to the duties we know about, she probably undertook other tasks, paid or unpaid, that were private and confidential like the Dilke affair and have left no record. Trolling the British Newspaper Archive reveals a couple of cases where she served as executor of someone's will, but those small-print advertisements do not reveal whether that service was professional or personal.

There is, as far as I know, only one instance of another university-trained woman lawyer remarking on Eliza Orme's career, and that was Cornelia Sorabji, the first woman to study law at Oxford University, where she wrote the Bachelor of Civil Law examination in 1892. As I mentioned above, the Indian woman purposely distanced herself from the apparent impropriety of becoming 'a kind of Miss Orme' involved with an ugly divorce. Sorabji regarded herself as 'A Tory of the Tories', and cultivated members of the British aristocracy, while Orme might equally have been called 'a Liberal of the Liberals' and spent her time among aesthetes and intellectuals. It is not difficult to imagine that, in the late 1890s, the two women were rivals at a personal and cultural level, if not in professional practice (Sorabji returned to India after Oxford and primarily did social work among women living in seclusion (*purdahnashins*). Mary Jane Mossman has written a useful essay about the intersection of gender, race, and political ideology in Sorabji's career.

Nor do I know how much money Eliza Orme made from her various paid jobs. They were highly specialized, and the work was in demand, so she probably did well, but her prosperity might still have been unstable. But the LL.B. did stand her in good stead. It was a credential that opened the door to gainful, if rather precarious, employment not available to other women. In the Liberal Party, the degree gave her credibility with the men, as well as the women.

Nevertheless, Eliza Orme's reputation has been hampered by her status as the first woman in England to earn a law degree. That was an accident, but it got presented at the time and later as though it were some kind of victory. In the first place, Britain was far behind other countries in this regard, with women studying and practicing law elsewhere far earlier. More significantly, her degree preceded the first cohort of accredited, practicing, woman lawyers in Britain by three decades. A feminist analysis of such dubious achievements came almost a century later. Matilda Butler and William Paisley remarked in their 1980 book *Women and the Mass Media*: 'We are well into the age of the FW2. By patronizing the continuing struggle of women and by minimizing the distance from FW2 to HW2 ('Hundredth woman to ...'), these newspaper articles create an illusion of progress'. So, too, do historical accounts that conceal the realities of rebuff, frustration, and disappointment. To fit the FW2 stereotype, Eliza Orme's career narrative should have begun with a struggle to obtain the law degree, followed by some sort of practice that would justify the effort and make a coherent story. But in reality the degree itself was no great challenge. The setbacks were located in a system that did not change as quickly as she may have hoped it would.

Who Was She to Posterity?

Someone once told me that, in my writing, I needed to get rid of 'negative theorizing'—such as starting every other sentence with 'despite'. I feel as though I am still indulging in that bad rhetorical habit with this book: she is important, but she is not getting a full-fledged biography here, just a research memoir. She is more than an adjunct to Mill, Gladstone, or Gissing, but I can understand how she got that reputation. She was not a factory inspector or a prison authority; in fact she positioned herself above those occupations as an expert advisor. She is not someone whose feminism failed at a crucial moment; it was her adversaries who portrayed her that way. She forged a life and career that was so exceptional—so unthinkable—that her contemporaries did not know what to make of it. Each individual and group tried to fit her into categories that made sense in the context of their own limited understanding. For Mill, she was a safe pair of hands, someone without 'that feverish bustle' he associated with other women in politics. Gladstone does not seem to have left his impression, although he probably knew who she was. For Gissing, she was 'one of the busiest women living' but he did not seem to know what she was busy doing, and never bothered to preserve the many letters she wrote to him. For all the men who shared the *British Weekly* writer's belief that women would inevitably 'sensationalize' a social problem or waste the time of an important government commission by offering 'loose' or 'irrelevant' evidence, she was a valued exception to their patriarchal assumptions. Those who did not understand about the legal profession thought she was the first woman barrister. Politicians and others who did understand it were still not sure what went on behind the brass plaque in Chancery Lane, but they knew her journalism and activism. Lawyers who knew exactly what happened in those chambers were pleased to take discreet advantage of her professional services, especially since they could be passed off as one's own work. In the public realm, everybody understood her in relation to their own place in the world. In private, too, she was a friend, a daughter, a sister, an aunt, a cousin.

I have characterized Eliza Orme as an independent single professional woman in public life. Another way of saying this is that she was not the wife, daughter (or stepdaughter), or sister of a prominent man. Because of the way that archival preservation works, this negative status posed a problem for her impact on posterity. She played only a minor role in the lives of Samuel Alexander and George Gissing whose surviving papers capture some of her activities, whereas she might have been hugely important to W.A. Hunter, but he does not seem to have left much behind in the way of an archive. In any case, those three men were not at the social level of the Earl of Carlisle, John Stuart Mill, or W.E. Gladstone. The women associated with men like that have captured the attention of historians, not just because of their activities but because their papers were safely preserved along with those of their prominent family member. Rosalind Howard, Helen Taylor, Mary Drew (née Gladstone) and many others are important in their own right; but they are knowable because they can be identified and accorded the scholarship they deserve. For Orme, the absence of a defining relationship with a male who has captured the attention of historians is significant.

My own relationship to her has been rather like the one between biographer and subject in Alison Lurie's 1988 novel, *The Truth about Lorin Jones*. The biographer, Polly Alter, starts out half in love with her subject, gradually becomes disillusioned and alienated, then ends up recognizing the other woman's essential unknowability, finally deciding to write 'the real story ... the whole truth about Lorin Jones, with all the contradictions left in'. In Eliza Orme's life and work, the contradictions lie in the way the various elements fit together, or do not fit. I think her feminism was tempered by her Liberalism, and vice-versa. I believe her heritage of class privilege was tempered by close observation of working-class lives, and vice-versa. I think her strategic brilliance was tempered by an impatience that made her unsympathetic to people who should have been allies. There really was no one like her, and that makes it difficult to know how to assess the choices she made.

To me, Orme's career narrative only makes sense for someone so 'hopelessly practical' and obviously ambitious if I let myself imagine the way she expected the story to start, and how she wanted it to end. My guess is that she assumed legalization of women's suffrage and candidacy for parliamentary election would happen in the 1870s or 1880s, in time for her to step in and claim the prize. From that perspective, her activities make sense, from 1872 when she was twenty-three and wrote her letter to Helen Taylor, to 1892 when she was forty-three and had to abandon the leadership of the Women's Liberal Federation, to a few years later when it became clear that the Royal Commission opportunity was not going to lead to anything more substantial either. If she had indeed become the first woman Member of Parliament or first woman cabinet minister in the 1890s, then her choices in the earlier decades would look eminently reasonable. She set out with a plan to use her talents and intellect in the same way that men of her generation did. She was loyal, disciplined, well-connected, and level-headed.

Put that way, the legal work in Chancery Lane was not an end, it was a means to an end. If Eliza Orme ever told anyone she aimed to be an elected Member of Parliament, the evidence is lost. And perhaps she never said it, even to Reina or Beatrice, and my guess is wrong. Either way, fitting the elements together is my decision, and I claim the right both to speculate and to ground the research in my own experience of doing it. For me, 'the real story' is not the whole truth, but rather this fragmented narrative based on rigorous scholarship but inevitably laced with both guesswork and memoir.

Appendices

Acknowledgements

Most of my thanks go to the handful of people who have helped me conceptualize and realize the Eliza Orme project during these past few years, since I retired from the University of Windsor and through the Covid-19 pandemic. First among these is Mary Jane Mossman, whose staunch support and enthusiasm have heartened me when the enterprise seemed impossible. Mary Jane got interested in Orme long ago, for her own book on the first women lawyers in six different jurisdictions. She rejoiced with me when the photograph came to light and the Alexander letters turned up and she offered wise advice on matters of legal practice and feminist history-writing. Next comes my first reader, Heidi Jacobs, who helped me understand what kind of a book this is. When someone with Heidi's breadth of experience—novelist, librarian, writer of creative nonfiction—says your book is publishable, you believe her. I learned about the legal profession—and much else—from Myra Tawfik, Bill Bogart, and other friends in the Faculty of Law at the University of Windsor. Lorraine Janzen Kooistra was another scholar-friend who cheered the project along, advising on all matters Pre-Raphaelite, and suggesting the strategy that led to finding the missing volume of the *Women's Gazette*. I'm grateful, too, for the comments from two anonymous reviewers secured by Open Book Publishers, and especially for the strong support of Managing Director Alessandra Tosi and her team at OBP.

Formal—and heartfelt—acknowledgements are due to the staff of the British Library, the Women's Library at the London School of Economics, the John Rylands Library at the University of Manchester, and of the library of the University of Oregon at Eugene. All of them helped, either by service in person or by providing digital copies of documents. I am grateful to John Partington for family permission to use the image of Reina Lawrence, and to the National Portrait Gallery and the British Museum for making several other portrait images available. My gratitude to the late Pierre Coustillas for facilitating my access to the portrait of Eliza Orme herself is recorded in the text. Apart from libraries and archives as such, much of the backbone of the book, especially the genealogical record of the Orme, Lawrence, and Alexander families comes from intense and repeated study of the United Kingdom census records, which I've accessed (for a fee) through the Find My Past website. In addition, the British Newspaper Archive has given me numerous snippets of information about Orme's public life and the public response to her career. It feels a bit odd, but I also have to acknowledge the utility of Google, Wikipedia, and the Internet Archive: without them, much of the knowledge in this book would be inaccessible to me, locked as it is in obscure Victorian memoirs and in the handlists of archival collections.

My family have supported the project not least by setting up a way of living that allowed me to flourish intellectually in retirement and through the pandemic. Love and gratitude now to my daughter Jessica Kamphorst and son-in-law Alex Whitehead, and always to my beloved late husband Neil Campbell, who knew as much about Miss Orme and her associates as he did about my university colleagues.

Documentation

Because I wanted to write in as accessible and attractive a way as I could manage, I made the decision to write this book without footnotes, but in such a way that scholars could find and follow up on the sources that I've discovered. Events like the Special Examination for Women in 1869 are well-documented and easy to find via an internet search. Census records and periodical publications are widely available though not always Open Access. Orme's relationships with well-known figures like the Rossettis, the Mill/Taylor family, the Gissings, and (to some extent) the Dilkes are documented in scholarship devoted to those people. In addition, my digital research has turned up several scraps of information, such as Frances Buss's expectation that Miss Orme would help with science classes at the Camden School, and Mabel Barltrop's use of nicknames for her cousins Eliza and Beatrice. Anyone who wants to follow up on these materials can find them the same way I did. When necessary I've indicated the source in the text; in other cases the proper documentation can be found in one of my own published articles or chapters on Orme, listed below. The important manuscript collections, especially the Samuel Alexander and Helen Taylor papers, are also listed, along with all the other Orme letters that I know of.

Throughout the book I try to place the evidence in context and avoid confusion, as every good historian does. In many situations, Eliza Orme is mentioned in passing, in the context of another figure's activities or statements or decisions. It's been difficult to sort out just what is meant, for example when we learn that she insisted that the two daughters of George Bradlaugh not be allowed to join the Somerville Club. The paragraph where that is mentioned is one about a whole list of grievances and perceived slights on the part of one of those daughters. Orme's motives for her action, if indeed she took it, remain inaccessible. Sometimes these passing mentions can lead to misunderstanding, as with the suggestion that Eliza Orme senior was governess to Elizabeth Barrett Browning; that was a different Mrs Orme. I can also attest that the contemporary writer and educator Temple Augustus Orme was not a member of the family and nor was Edith Temple Orme, another student of law. There is even another public figure called Miss Eliza Orme, a missionary teacher who worked in India; her dates were 1882–1975.

Some evidence of identity was too frail for me to use, while others brought me to a dead end. In the first category, there is a Beatrice Helen Novelli (1855–1923) who married one Henry Glanville Southwell, a lawyer, in 1888, and had nine children (according to genealogical records). She might be the 'Miss Novelli' mentioned in the 1884 letter to Susan B. Anthony, who worked in Chancery Lane and departed with Mary Ellen Richardson to do business in Bedford Park, but there could easily be more than one 'Miss Novelli' in London. In the dead-end category, sadly, is the Beatrice Orme went on an archaeological dig to Egypt in 1898–90, working with her friend Hilda Petrie. That would have been a very satisfying connection, but Eliza's sister Beatrice was 41 in 1898, too old to be the short-skirted adventurer in Petrie's photograph and an unlikely fourteen years older than Hilda. Anyway, again, there are others in census records with the same name.

Finally, and contrary to some online accounts, my subject's name was Eliza, not Elizabeth. I can confirm that I have copies of both birth and death certificates to this effect.

Major Figures, and Families

Alexander, Samuel 1859–1938. Philosopher. Born in Australia, moved to England 1877; joined by his family 1892. Appointed Professor at Owens College, Manchester 1893.

Andrews, Edward 1787–1841. Congregational minister living in Walworth, south London. Married 1811 to Elizabeth Honour Andrews 1792–1831. Twelve children including Eliza Orme's mother and aunts: Eliza Orme (1816–1892), Emily Augusta Patmore (1824–1862), and Georgina Patmore (born ca 1826).

Bastian, Julia Augusta 1840–1928 (née Orme; married 1866 to Henry Charlton Bastian 1837–1915). Lived in London. Five children (May Bastian, later Strick 1868–1904; Charles Orme Bastian 1869–1924; James Bastian 1874–1934?; William Bastian 1875–1937; Sybil Bastian 1879–1961).

Collet, Clara 1860–1948. Teacher, economist and civil servant. BA and MA from University College London; worked with Charles Booth on his investigation of social conditions. Later she was one of the lady assistant commissioners on the Royal Commission on Labour and worked with Eliza Orme to support George Gissing.

Deane, Lucy 1865–1950. One of the first women factory inspectors in the UK. Information about the advice Deane received from Orme comes from a novel by Lisa Wright, *A Most Unladylike Occupation: Lucy Deane, the First Female Factory Inspector 1890s* (Market Harborough: Book Guild Publishing Ltd, 2018). Wright drew upon Deane's unpublished diaries which are lodged at the British Library of Political and Economic Science at the London School of Economics. I have not seen these diaries.

Fox, Olivia Blanche 1844–1930 (née Orme; married 1864 to Howard Fox 1836–1922). Lived in Cornwall. Four children (Howard Orme Fox 1865–1921; Charles Masson Fox 1866–1935; Olivia Lloyd Fox 1868–1935; Stella Fox 1876–1954).

Ghose, Manomohan 1844–1896. First practicing barrister born in India. Called to the bar at Lincoln's Inn 1866. One of his cases is featured in Orme's *Trial of Shama Charan Pal* (1897).

Gissing, George 1857–1903. Novelist; married first to Nell Harrison (1879) then to Edith Underwood (1891) and partnership with Gabrielle Fleury (from 1898). Two children with Edith (Walter Leonard Gissing 1891–1916 and Alfred Charles Gissing 1896–1975). Orme assisted with his separation from Edith and support of the children. Gissing did not preserve her many letters to him.

Lawrence, Emily Asher 1832–1912 (née Asher, first married name Mills); married to John Moss Lawrence (1825/6–1888). Born Spanish Town, Jamaica. Nine children (Laurie Asher Lawrence 1857–1949; Arthur Moss Lawrence 1859–1933; Reina Emily Lawrence 1868–1940; Esther Ella ('Essie') Lawrence 1862–1944; Caroline Lawrence 1864/5–??; Alice L. Lawrence 1866/7–??; Henry Walton ('Harry') Lawrence 1869–1937; Amy Lilian Lawrence 1871–??; Gerald Leslie Lawrence 1873–1957).

Lawrence, Henry Walton ('Harry') 1869–1937. Partner in Lawrence & Bullen, publishers from 1891 to about 1900. Later worked for the Medici Society.

Lawrence, Reina Emily 1861–1940. LL.B. University College London 1893. Second business partner and lifelong friend of Eliza Orme. First woman elected as a borough councillor in London, 1907–1909. Active in Women's National Liberal Association. The photograph of Lawrence was printed in a pamphlet entitled 'Hampstead Borough Council Election. MONDAY NEXT, NOVEMBER 1ST, 1909', which is held in Camden Local Studies and Archives Centre.

Masson, Emily Rosaline 1835–1915 (née Orme; married 1854 to David Masson 1822–1907). Active in Edinburgh women's suffrage movement. Four children (Flora Masson 1856–1937; David Orme Masson 1858–1937;

Helen Orme Masson (later Gulland) 1863–1963, Rosaline Masson 1867–1947).

Orme, Beatrice Masson 1857–1949. Student at University College London but apparently did not graduate. Active in Women's Liberal Association and later Women's National Liberal Association.

Orme, Campbell 1842–1883. Medical Officer. Died Rio de Janeiro.

Orme, Charles Edward 1833–1912. Surgeon (Member of the Royal College of Surgeons).

Orme, Eliza (senior) 1816–1892 (née Andrews; married 1832 to the distiller Charles Orme 1806–1893). Active in London women's suffrage movement. Patron of the arts, in particular of the Pre-Raphaelites. Daughter of Rev. Edward Andrews; sister of Emily Patmore and Georgina Patmore. Eight children (Charles Edward Orme, Emily Rosaline Orme (later Masson), Helen Foster Orme, Julia Augusta Orme (later Bastian), Campbell Orme, Olivia Blanche Orme (later Fox), Eliza Orme, Beatrice Masson Orme).

Orme, Eliza 1848–1937. Legal practitioner, Liberal politician, a Director of the Nineteenth Century Building Society, editor of *Women's Gazette & Weekly News*, investigator of labour and prison conditions.

Orme, Helen Foster 1836–1857. Friend of Christina Rossetti.

Patmore family; see Andrews.

Richardson, Mary Ellen. Dates unknown, born ca 1840–1845. Studied law at University College but apparently did not graduate. Hon. Treasurer of the Association to Promote Women's Knowledge of Law. First business partner of Eliza Orme and a Director of the Nineteenth Century Building Society. Elected to London School Board 1879–1885. Lived with Jane Chessar. From about 1884, manager of The Stores, Bedford Park, later principal shareholder and director. Moved to The Lizard, Cornwall in 1894, served as parish councillor.

Eliza Orme: A Partial Bibliography

Correspondence (Manuscript and Print)

Letters to Samuel Alexander. Alexander Papers, John Rylands Library, University of Manchester. Eighteen letters dated 1886 to 1916, some undated. GB133 ALEX/A/1/216.

Letter to Susan B. Anthony, 26 February 1884. Published in National Woman Suffrage Association. Report of the Sixteenth Annual Washington Convention, March 1884. Library of Congress. https://tile.loc.gov/storage-services/service/rbc/rbnawsa/n8341/n8341.pdf

Letter to Clara Collet about Edith Gissing. 29 December 1897. Reproduced in Pierre Coustillas, *The Heroic Life of George Gissing*. Vol. 3, 2014: p. 48.

Letters to Talfourd Ely responding to Pascoe Daphne's protest, 9 and 11 January 1877. University College London Library Special Collections. File includes also letters from Pascoe Daphne to Sheldon Amos and others, dated November-December 1876.

Letter to Richard Garnett, 19 May 1873. Harry Ransom Center, University of Texas at Austin.

Letter to William Stanley Jevons, 14 March 1881, informing him of an error in his *Elementary Lessons in Logic*. Jevons Family Papers, John Rylands Library, University of Manchester. GB133 JA/6/1.

Letter to Miss Ridley, 18 September 1874. London School of Economics. Women's Library Archive. Autograph Letter Collection: Female Education. Seeking recommendation of a school with instruction of an advanced kind. This is presumably Annie E. Ridley (1839–1923, novelist and school administrator). GB 106 9/04/18.

Letters to Harriet Taylor, and drafts of Taylor's replies. Mill-Taylor collection. London School of Economics Library, British Library of Political and Economic Science. Nineteen letters dated 1872–1875.

Letter to the Editor, *Women's Gazette & Weekly News*, headed 'The Ethics of Public Life', signed EO (30 November 1889; continued the following week).

Letter to the Editor, *Pall Mall Gazette*, signed as Editor of *WGWN*, concerning Dilke (24 November 1891).

Letter from the Editor, *WGWN* (i.e. E. Orme), 7 December 1891, referring to *WGWN* policy with respect to publishing comment from the 'progressive' faction.

Letter to the Editor, *WGWN*, 12 April 1892, satirizing Nora Philipps's article in the Welsh Review and recommending Jevons's *Elements of Logic* to recognize a fallacy.

Letter to the Editor, *WGWN*, 30 August, 1892, concerning the dispute within the Women's Liberal Federation.

Eliza Orme's Known Publications (in Chronological Order)

'University Degrees for Women', *The Examiner* (16 May 1874), p. 508. Signed Eliza Orme.

'University Degrees for Women', *The Examiner* (4 July 1874), pp. 707–08. Signed E.O.

'Sound Minded Women', *The Examiner* (1 August 1874), pp. 820–21. Signed E.O.

'Song', *The Examiner* (31 July 1875), p.13. Signed E.O. Poem.

'Women in College', *One and All: A Journal for Everybody* (September 1880). I have not seen this item, which has apparently not been digitized. Advertised in the *Weekly Dispatch* on 19 September. This may be the 'obnoxious article' referred to by Eliza Savage in her 21 September letter to Samuel Butler (although that may also refer to 'A New Club for Women' published anonymously in the same newspaper in August 1880, except that it contains nothing particularly obnoxious).

'Matilda Chaplin Ayrton, MD', *Englishwoman's Review* (15 August 1883), p. 343.

'Jeanette Wilkinson', *Englishwoman's Review* (15 September 1886), p. 385.

'Women's Work in Creation. A Reply', *Longman's Magazine* (December 1886), pp. 149–158.

Index to Savill Vaizey, *A Treatise on the Law of Settlements of Property, Made Upon Marriage and Other Occasions.* 2 volumes. (London: H. Sweet and Co., et al, 1887).

Various leading articles, *Weekly Dispatch*. Possibly 1887–1892, the period coinciding with W. A. Hunter's editorship of that newspaper.

Various editorials, *Women's Gazette and Weekly News*. From 7 September 1889 to 7 March 1892, Orme served as Editor of the weekly newspaper (which later appeared monthly). Regular editorials/leaders were published anonymously and cannot be identified with precision. Identifiable articles and letters are cited below.

'Parted', *Women's Gazette and Weekly News* (26 July 1890). Unsigned poem; text almost identical to 'Song' in 1875 *Examiner*.

'A Clear Issue', *Women's Gazette and Weekly News* (15 June 1891). Supplement to *WGWN*, signed essay on Women's Liberal Federation politics.

'Women as Politicians', *East Anglian Daily Times* (12 February 1892). Part of a series by several 'Representative Women on Questions Social and Political'.

'A Commonplace Correction', *Welsh Review* (March 1892). Reply to Nora Philipps's article with respect to Women's Liberal Federation's suffrage policy ('The Problem of the Nineteenth Century').

'On the Condition of Women in the Nail, Chain and Bolt Making Industries in the Black Country'. Parliamentary Paper 36 (1892), Vol. II., *Minutes of Evidence, Group A*, pp. 569–75. See also 1895 report listed below.

The Employment of Women. Reports by Miss Eliza Orme, Miss Clara E. Collet, Miss May E. Abraham, and Miss Margaret H. Irwin (Lady Assistant Commissioners) on the Conditions of Work in Various Industries in England, Wales, Scotland, and Ireland. (London: Eyre and Spottiswoode, 1893).

'The Legal Status of Women in England', *The Albany Law Journal* (19 August 1893), p. 8.

'The Employment of Women. Report by Eliza Orme (Senior Assistant Commissioner) on the Condition of Women in the Nail, Chain, and Bolt Making Industries in the "Black Country".' *Minutes of Evidence, with Appendices, Taken before Group 'A' of the Royal Commission on Labour* (Volume II) *Mining*. Presented to both houses of Parliament, June 1892, pp. 569–75. Published 1895.

The Trial of Shama Charan Pal: An Illustration of Village Life in Bengal (London: Lawrence & Bullen, 1897). https://archive.org/details/in.ernet. dli.2015.283821/page/n5/mode/2up

'How Poor Ladies Live: A Reply'. *Nineteenth Century* (April 1897, vol. 41, no. 242).

'Sketch of Lady Fry'. *British Weekly* (May 1897); reprinted in other papers.

Lady Fry of Darlington (London: Hodder & Stoughton, 1898). https://archive. org/details/ladyfrydarlingt00ormegoog/mode/2up

' Our Female Criminals'. *Fortnightly Review* (May, 1898), pp. 790–96.

'William Alexander Hunter', *Dictionary of National Biography. Supplement.* Ed. Sidney Lee (London: Macmillan, 1901). https://doi.org/10.1093/ ref:odnb/14236

'Samuel Plimsoll', *Dictionary of National Biography. Supplement.* Ed. Sidney Lee (London: Macmillan, 1901). https://doi.org/10.1093/ref:odnb/22384.

'Thomas Bayley Potter', *Dictionary of National Biography. Supplement.* Ed. Sidney Lee (London: Macmillan, 1901). https://doi.org/10.1093/ref:odnb/22621

Publications about Eliza Orme

'A Group of Liberal Dames', *British Weekly*, 3 March 1892. Reprinted in *Women's Gazette and Weekly News*, 12 April 1892. Anonymous, but possibly attributable to William Robertson Nicoll.

Howsam, Leslie, 'Eliza Orme and the *Women's Gazette and Weekly News*: Editing the Organ of a Fractious Federation, 1888–92', *Victorian Periodicals Review* 55, 1 (Spring 2022), 100–124. https://doi.org/10.1353/vpr.2022.0004

—, 'Legal Paperwork & Public Policy in Late-Victorian Britain: Eliza Orme's Professional Expertise', in *Precarious Professionals: Gender, Identities and Social Change in Modern Britain*, ed. Heidi Egginton and Zoë Thomas (London: University of London Press, 2021), 107–24. This Open Access volume also contains an essay by Ren Pepitone about the masculine culture of the Inns of Court. https://www.sas.ac.uk/publications/precarious-professionals https://doi.org/10.14296/202110.9781912702633

—, 'Eliza Orme, 1848–1937', *The Dictionary of National Biography Missing Persons*, ed. C. S. Nicholls (Oxford: Oxford University Press, 1993), 505–06. Updated and expanded in subsequent online editions of the *Oxford Dictionary of National Biography*. https://doi.org/10.1093/ref:odnb/37825

—, '"Sound-Minded Women:" Eliza Orme and the Study and Practice of Law in Late-Victorian England', *Atlantis: A Women's Studies Journal* 15, 1 (1989), 44–55. https://journals.msvu.ca/index.php/atlantis/article/view/5125/4323

Mossman, Mary Jane, *The First Women Lawyers: A Comparative Study of Gender, Law and the Legal Professions* (Oxford: Hart Publishing, 2006). Chapter 3: '"Sound Women" and Legal Work: the First Women in Law in Britain'.

—, 'Precedents, Patterns and Puzzles: Feminist Reflections on the First Women Lawyers', *Laws* 5, 4 (2016), 1–17. https://doi.org/10.3390/laws5040039

Robson, Ann. 'Legal Proof of [John Stuart Mill's] Dissertations and Discussions', *Mill News Letter* (Summer 1976), pp. 22–25. https://www.ucl.ac.uk/bentham-project/sites/bentham_project/files/Mill011-2.pdf.

Index

About the Team

Alessandra Tosi was the managing editor for this book.

Annie Hine was in charge of proofreading this manuscript; Adèle Kreager indexed it.

The Alt-text was created by the author.

Jeevanjot Kaur Nagpal designed the cover. The cover was produced in InDesign using the Fontin font.

Cameron Craig typeset the book in InDesign and produced the paperback and hardback editions. The text font is Tex Gyre Pagella and the heading font is Californian FB.

Cameron also produced the PDF, EPUB, XML and HTML editions. The conversion was performed with open-source software and other tools freely available on our GitHub page at https://github.com/OpenBookPublishers.

This book need not end here...

Share

All our books — including the one you have just read — are free to access online so that students, researchers and members of the public who can't afford a printed edition will have access to the same ideas. This title will be accessed online by hundreds of readers each month across the globe: why not share the link so that someone you know is one of them?

This book and additional content is available at:
https://doi.org/10.11647/OBP.0392

Donate

Open Book Publishers is an award-winning, scholar-led, not-for-profit press making knowledge freely available one book at a time. We don't charge authors to publish with us: instead, our work is supported by our library members and by donations from people who believe that research shouldn't be locked behind paywalls.

Why not join them in freeing knowledge by supporting us:
https://www.openbookpublishers.com/support-us

Follow @OpenBookPublish

Read more at the Open Book Publishers **BLOG**

You may also be interested in:

Margery Spring Rice
Pioneer of Women's Health in the Early Twentieth Century
Lucy Pollard

https://doi.org/10.11647/obp.0215

Breaking Conventions
**Five Couples in Search of Marriage-Career Balance at
the Turn of the Nineteenth Century**
Patricia Auspos

https://doi.org/10.11647/obp.0318

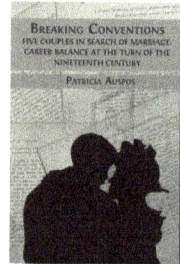

Susan Isaacs
A Life Freeing the Minds of Children
Philip Graham

https://doi.org/10.11647/obp.0297

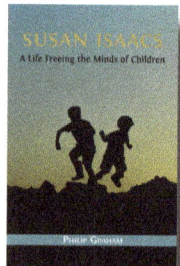

www.ingramcontent.com/pod-product-compliance
Lightning Source LLC
Chambersburg PA
CBHW050809270326
41926CB00026B/4650